SCRIPTURE UNION

BIBLE CHARACTERS AND DOCTRINES

The Shepherd to Judas
E. M. BLAIKLOCK, M.A., D.Litt.

Life in Christ
J. I. PACKER, M.A., D.Phil.

SCRIPTURE UNION
5 WIGMORE STREET
LONDON, W1H OAD

© 1974 Scripture Union
First Published 1974

ISBN 0 85421 314 7

Printed and bound in England by
Cox & Wyman Ltd, London, Reading and Fakenham

INTRODUCTION

This series of S.U. Bible study aids takes its place alongside our existing range of Notes and Bible Study Books.

Each volume of Bible Characters and Doctrines is divided into the right number of sections to make daily use possible, though dates are not attached to the sections because of the books' continuing use as a complete set of character studies and doctrinal expositions. The study for each day is clearly numbered and the Bible passage to be read is placed alongside it.

Sections presenting the characters and doctrines alternate throughout each book, providing balance and variety in the selected subjects. At the end of each section there is a selection of questions and themes for further study related to the material covered in the preceding readings.

Each volume will provide material for one quarter's use, with between 91 and 96 sections. Where it is suggested that two sections should be read together in order to fit the three-month period, they are marked with an asterisk.

The scheme will be completed in four years. Professor E. M. Blaiklock, who writes all the character studies, will work progressively through the Old and New Testament records. Writers of the doctrinal sections contribute to a pattern of studies drawn up by the Rev. Geoffrey Grogan, Principal of the Bible Training Institute, Glasgow, in his capacity as Co-ordinating Editor. A chart overleaf indicates how the doctrinal sections are planned.

In this series biblical quotations are normally taken from the RSV unless otherwise identified. Occasionally Professor Blaiklock provides his own translation of the biblical text.

DOCTRINAL STUDY SCHEME

	Year 1	Year 2	Year 3	Year 4
First Quarter	The God who Speaks	Man and Sin	The Work of Christ	The Kingdom and the Church
Second Quarter	God in His World	Law and Grace	Righteousness in Christ	The Mission of the Church
Third Quarter	The Character of God	The Life of Christ	Life in Christ	The Church's Ministry and Ordinances
Fourth Quarter	The Holy Trinity	The Person of Christ	The Holy Spirit	The Last Things

DOCTRINAL STUDIES
LIFE IN CHRIST

Study

Regeneration

1	A New Heart	Deuteronomy 30.1–10; Jeremiah 31.31–34; Ezekiel 36.25–27
2	You must be Born Again	John 3.1–15
3	New Birth Shows Itself	John 1.9–13; 1 John 3.1–10
4	Imperishable Seed- Imperishable Hope	1 Peter 1.3–5; 1.22–2.3
5	Risen with Christ	Ephesians 2.1–10

The Pattern Life

12	The Ten Commandments	Exodus 20.1–17
13	Portrait of a Happy Man	Matthew 5.1–12
14	An Example	John 13.1–20
15	The Greatest Thing	1 Corinthians 13
16	Hope and Holiness	1 Peter 1.13–21
17	In His Steps	1 Peter 2.18–25

Identification with Christ

26	The Way of the Cross	Mark 8.31–38; Galatians 2.20; 6.11–18
27	Risen, Freed and Enslaved	Romans 6
28	Holding Fast the Head	Colossians 2.6–19
29	Christ is our Life	Colossians 2.20–3.15

Growth in Grace

35	Abide in Christ	John 15.1–17
36	Knowing and Growing	Ephesians 1.15–23; 3.14–21
37	Man of One Thing	Philippians 3
38	Practical Holiness	1 Thessalonians 3.11–4.12

Study

The Word of God and Life in Christ

Prayer and Life in Christ

The Indwelling Spirit

Christian Fellowship

Study
The Christian in the World

CHARACTER STUDIES
THE SHEPHERD TO JUDAS

LIFE IN CHRIST

Introduction

The following studies deal with what Paul calls *new creation* (2 Cor. 5.17; Gal. 6.15)—'the life of God in the soul of man', to quote the title of Henry Scougal's book which helped the Wesleys and Whitefield to see what Christianity really is. The text-book names for the themes involved are regeneration and sanctification; personal means of grace (prayer, the Bible, fellowship); and the Christian calling. Older divines spoke of the work of the Holy Spirit in the application of redemption.

To deal with our new life in Christ is to walk a tight-rope off which it is easy to fall to both the right and the left: and either way of falling can be ruinous. The Bible view is that before regeneration we are bondslaves of sin; after regeneration we are free from sin's dominion, though not from its counter-attacks and sabotaging action; in heaven, however, we shall be free from its presence, for it will be rooted out of us entirely. Thus total renewal is promised, starting here and completed hereafter. Perfectionists affirm too much, for they maintain that sin may be wholly eradicated or suppressed here and now—which leads in practice, always and necessarily, to an inadequate view of sin. Usually, however, perfectionists are reacting against a commoner error, that of affirming too little, and expecting no transformation of character in this world—which reflects all too clearly an inadequate view of grace. Both mistakes must be avoided. The passage set for study will help us here.

Since life in Christ was on the whole better understood and expounded in the past than nowadays it is, the following list of books for background and supplementary reading contains several old items:

J. Murray, *Redemption Accomplished and Applied* (Banner of Truth)

A. M. Stibbs and J. I. Packer, *The Spirit Within You* (Hodders)

J. C. Ryle, *Holiness*; *Practical Religion*; *Old Paths* (all James Clarke)

W. Marshall, *The Gospel Mystery of Sanctification* (Marshalls)

J. Bunyan, *The Pilgrim's Progress from This World to the Next*

LIFE IN CHRIST

Regeneration

1 : A New Heart

Deuteronomy 30.1–10; Jeremiah 31.31–34; Ezekiel 36.25–27

Scripture views sin as a racial fact, the essence of which is that *man plays God* (see Gen. 3.5f.). Sin estranges us from our Maker, evoking His wrath against our disobedience and destroying our power to heed His word (cf. Rom. 8.6–8; 1 Cor. 2.14). God, however, has taken action. By sending His Son into the world to be the propitiation for our sins (1 John 4.10) He has opened the door to pardon, reconciliation, and restored fellowship. Now by sending His Spirit into our hearts He restores responsiveness, so that we actually pass through this door by faith in Christ (cf. John 6.44f.; 10.25–28). Titus 3.5 calls this inner renewing *regeneration*.

Today's three passages speak of God restoring His people from captivity, which is His 'curse' (Deut. 30.1) on them for breaking His covenant (29.25ff.). All three declare that in faithfulness to His covenant purpose and love for His covenant people God will bring them back to their land and their Lord. Circumcision signified God's covenant commitment to Israel, and His covenant claim upon them; hence, when Deut. 30.6 (cf. v. 8) speaks of God as circumcising Israelite hearts so that they love Him wholly, the meaning is that God will cause covenant communion between Him and them to be fully realized and enjoyed. This is exactly what God predicts through Jeremiah: a day when He will renew covenant fellowship between Himself and Israel, not by ceasing to be their 'husband', but by deepening His work of grace—that is, by so changing their hearts that all will obey Him and know Him and taste His pardoning love. The promise concluding v. 33 is the 'slogan' of God's covenant throughout the Bible and at every stage of God's plan (see Gen. 17.7f.; Exod. 6.7; Zech. 8.8; 2 Cor. 6.16; Rev. 21.3). It means that all God is and has is for His people (Rom. 8.31); and all they are and have must be for Him. The fulfilment of Jeremiah's prophecy through Christ is announced in Heb. 8.6–13 and 10.11–18. Ezekiel's prediction echoes Jeremiah's, adding (1) that God works this inner renewal by His Spirit and (2) that His renewing of their hearts is a purging from defilement. The thought here is that sin has made us inwardly dirty, and we need cleansing (25, cf. Psa. 51.7).

Thus God works regeneration in His almighty love, renewing the heart (not the physical organ, but the inner man, the real deep down you and me). In this way a life of faith and godliness becomes natural, whereas before it was impossible. So human nature *can* be changed!—praise God! ✓

2 : You must be Born Again

John 3.1–15

Nicodemus came to Jesus as spokesman for the Pharisaic theological circle in Jerusalem (the 'we' of v. 2 and the plural 'you' of vs. 7, 11f.), apparently to invite the young country rabbi into the fellowship of this learned society—in other words, to patronize Jesus. But Jesus would not relate to him on that basis. The abruptness of v. 3 as a response to the politeness of v. 2 reflects, not rudeness, but a radical discernment of need. Without new birth, says Jesus, none can see or enter the Kingdom of God. In Jesus' preaching, the Kingdom appears as a complex of relationships whereby those who live under His rule enjoy God's forgiveness and fatherly care. The Pharisees were looking for God's Kingdom; Jesus is telling Nicodemus that the Kingdom already exists, but those not born again can neither detect its presence nor share its life.

'New birth' is one of Jesus' 'earthly things' (12), i.e. His parables. (Parable means 'comparison'; metaphors as well as stories are parables.) The point of the parable is that regeneration is a completely new beginning. Nicodemus is at first bewildered through taking the parable literally (4), so Jesus explains that the 'birth' He means is 'of water and the Spirit' (5). His chiding of Nicodemus, 'a teacher of Israel', for not understanding this (10) implies that the new birth should be familiar to one who taught the Old Testament. This makes it natural to refer 'water and the Spirit', not to Christian baptism, or John's baptism, plus Pentecost (how could Jesus have expected Nicodemus to grasp a reference to that?), but to the two-sided work of inner renewal foretold in Ezek. 36.25–27. Jesus pictures this renewal to Nicodemus as a fresh birth, leading to a new Spirit-led life incomprehensible to those outside (8).

Note Jesus' progress of thought. Verses 3–8 say: Would you (i.e. you Pharisaic theologians, you self-appointed authorities on spiritual matters) see and enter the Kingdom of God? Then you must be born again. Verses 9–11 say: Would you be born again? Then you must receive our witness (i.e., Mine, and that of My disciples who already know the new birth and the life of the Kingdom first-hand). Verses 14f. say: Will you receive My witness? Then I tell you to put your faith in the heaven-sent Son of Man who, like the brazen serpent in Num. 21.9, is to be 'lifted up' as a means of life. When Jesus said 'lifted up' He was thinking forward to His crucifixion and exaltation (cf. 8.28; 12.32), though Nicodemus could only have understood 'lifted up' in the sense of being displayed as an object of attention. John 7.50 and 19.39 indicate, however, that light dawned for Nicodemus and he became a disciple.

3 : New Birth Shows Itself

John 1.9–13; 1 John 3.1–10

Without new birth God's approach draws no response from man. The first passage shows this. Taken from the prologue of John's Gospel, it tells us that the Word who came into the world by incarnation was already the source of the light of *general revelation*—inklings of God, His law, and His judgement—which everyone receives, willy-nilly. But we know from Paul that this light is regularly turned into darkness by closing 'the eyes of the heart' (Eph. 1.18) and giving oneself up to fantasies of various kinds (see Rom. 1.19–28). Verses 4f. of John's prologue point to this: the light of general revelation shines in darkness, and if the darkness could *suppress* it and *put it out* (the Greek word means this), it would.

Distinct from *general* revelation is *special* revelation of God's saving grace, which comes through knowledge of the Word incarnate. Verse 9 says that He who already gives general revelation came to be the medium of special revelation too. But man's reaction was the same. His own world, which He made, and His own people, the Jews, rejected Him. Once more the darkness sought to put out the light.

But some responded (12), and to these He gave the right

(better, *privilege*) of becoming God's sons—objects, that is, of God's fatherly care (cf. 20.17) and heirs of His glory (cf. 17.22; Rom. 8.17). How was it that they responded? Through being born of God, by a supernatural process distinct from natural birth (13: 'blood' signifies human parentage). Adoption is through faith; faith is through regeneration.

The second passage also moves from adoption (1–3) to the new birth which underlies it (9), and centres on the point that new birth necessarily produces a moral change, because God's 'seed' ('nature', RSV) remains in the regenerate. A reborn man does righteousness, i.e. God's revealed will (7, 10), and declines lawlessness, i.e. sin (4), just as Jesus did (5). The present tenses of vs. 6, 7, 8, 9, 10 have habitual rather than categorical force, as is common in Greek; the verbs in v. 9 should be translated 'commits sin habitually', 'cannot sin habitually'. Chapter 1.8–10 shows that John does not mean 'never sins'! John insists, however, that where there are no signs of the new life of righteousness (imitation of Christ, vs. 5–7; love of Christians, v. 10) there is no regeneration either, but a person is still the devil's child (10).

4 : Imperishable Seed—Imperishable Hope

1 Peter 1.3–5; 1.22–2.3

The 'living hope' of Christians (so called because it is vivid, and gives energy, and brings life eternal; cf. 'living word', v. 23) is the expectation of risen life with Christ at His 'revelation', i.e. His appearing (7). God's promise is of fellowship with their beloved Saviour (8) in His glory, making their salvation from sin and evil complete (4, 9, 10; 2.2). The adjectives 'imperishable, undefiled, unfading' (4) emphasize that this inheritance belongs to the order of heavenly things that abide, in contrast to the tainted and transient wealth of this world (cf. 1 Cor. 7.31; Matt. 6.19–21). Jesus's own resurrection is that on which this hope depends (3); the Christian's new birth, bringing him to faith in Christ (5, 8), is the means whereby it becomes his (3); and the protecting power of God is the guarantee that he will finally attain what he hopes for (5). These facts establish the joyful forward-looking mood that should mark all Christian living.

Chapter 1.22–2.3, which should be read as a single paragraph, has an ethical thrust. First Peter insists that those who share this hope should love their brothers and fellow heirs in God's family (cf. 3.7f.) with complete sincerity and with all their might (22). Peter's language is searching and challenging: do we love other Christians like that? Then he tells them to renounce the various forms of crooked living (2.1), and to long for 'pure spiritual milk' to make them grow into what they hope to be (2). The 'milk' is surely basic Christian teaching, given by God through the apostles and now found in the Bible (cf. 1 Cor. 3.2; Heb. 5.12f.). New-born babies crave intensely for their milk, as their crying shows; Christians should desire God's instruction with equal intensity. All Peter's demands here, together with his references to brothers and babies, flow from the thought of the new birth, which appears again in v. 23. 'Imperishable seed' (an image of begetting) declares that God's renewal of us by the Spirit lasts for ever, while the description of the 'everlasting gospel', the outward means which God used to bring us to faith, as 'abiding' assures us that the promises of salvation will never prove false.

5 : Risen with Christ

Ephesians 2.1–10

Apart from Titus 3.5, Paul does not speak of regeneration; his way of expressing the thought of new birth is to speak of *new creation* (10; 4.24; 2 Cor. 5.17) whereby the spiritually dead are made alive with Christ (1–7; Col. 2.13f.; Rom. 6.3–11).

Here, being *dead* (1, 5) signifies three things: (i) unresponsiveness to God (corpses do not answer when you address them); (ii) separation from God's fellowship, which is that 'life' for which we were made (2.12; 4.18, cf. John 17.3; Psa. 36.9); (iii) exposure to God's wrath (3)—that is, His present hostility and judgement to come (cf. 5.6). Those who are thus *dead* follow a course of life dictated by the world, the devil and the flesh, a life of disobedience to God (2f.). The Bible has a rich store of picture-words for this disobedience: 'trespasses' in Greek signifies false steps, blundering off the path God set us to walk on, and 'sins' is a picture of repeatedly missing the targets God set us to aim at. Note Paul's insistence in v. 3 that there is something guilty and twisted, self-deifying and anti-God, about all the 'drives' of our fallen nature, desires of the mind—'the lust of the eyes (coveting) and the pride of life' (1 John 2.16)—as well as desires seated in the body.

16

Concerning God's quickening of the spiritually dead, so saving them (5, 8), note:

1. It springs from *love*, *mercy*, *grace* and *kindness* so completely without parallel as to be largely beyond our thought. Paul piles up words speaking of the *wealth* and *greatness* of this love (4, 7f., cf. 1.5–8), only to confess finally that it is *immeasurable* and passes knowledge (7; 3.18f.).

2. It takes place *in Christ*, i.e. through the execution of God's eternal plan to make union with His incarnate Son the means of our salvation (1.3). Jesus Christ is the mediator to us of all God's gifts, including newness of life; 'the last Adam became a life-giving Spirit' (1 Cor. 15.45).

3. It catches us up into God's act of *raising Christ from the dead*. The Church is the extension, not of the incarnation, but of the resurrection. Those raised sit with Christ in the heavenlies (6), i.e. they enjoy a hidden life that puts them always 'on top', since He who is ruling the worlds makes all things work for their good (cf. Rom. 8.28).

4. A course of *God-planned obedience* is its goal (10).

It thus appears that our salvation through faith, first to last, is all God's doing, and in no sense ours (8f.); so all the praise for it must be His.

Questions and themes for study and discussion on Studies 1–5

1. What is the relation between new birth and justification?
2. Who are Nicodemus' modern equivalents?
3. Was the new birth a reality under the old covenant?
4. What are the signs that a person has been born again?
5. List the ingredients which make up the Christian hope.
6. How does Eph. 2.1–10 apply to persons who have been Christians as long as they can remember?

CHARACTER STUDIES

*6 : The Shepherd

John 10; Psalm 23

The image of the Shepherd, like all the word-pictures of the Bible, must be comprehended in its ancient context of time and place. The modern shepherd presents a blurred picture. In New Zealand the sheep far outnumber the human population. They are a white dust on the rolling green of Southland, as far as the eye can see. Their hardier breeds crop the mountain grasses far up the Southern Alps. But none of them knows its shepherd, nor is known to him by name. Dogs, uncannily trained to obey a whistle, herd and gather them. Mounted men drive the great billowing massed flocks to market. Pathetically patient, they stand in two-decked railway wagons, drawn in long rakes to the killing-place. If there is a picture of humanity here, it is the proletarian multitude of some dictator-ridden land, the herded hordes of totalitarian regimes.

The Eastern shepherd 'went before' his sheep. They knew his voice. This was part of the Lord's comprehensive imagery in John 10. And such was ancient shepherding. Even in Homer's tale of the Cyclops, the blinded giant sits in the cave door and knows the sheep under which the wily Odysseus had tied his men, even by the touch of his fingers. 'The Lord is our Shepherd', and it is thus that He knows us, individually, not in harassed mass.

Sheep are foolish creatures, prone to follow a leader blindly, apt to wander, pathetically human in their carelessness. A wall-scratching in the catacombs shows the Good Shepherd, a favourite theme for those first Christian artists. The sheep are around Him. Some rest at His feet. Others graze with heads turned away, others disappear over a ridge, tails just showing. Any pastor (and the word means shepherd) could thus classify his flock.

The helpless creatures demanded continual care. Thieves preyed upon them, climbing into the fold by 'some other way' than by the door; the wild beast lurked to 'scatter the flock'; the burdened and the sick demanded the shepherd's careful strength. On the rolling hills around Bethlehem the first pastoral poet saw the pathos and significance of it all, and found the imagery and truth of the Shepherd Psalm, that veritable gem of Hebrew and English literature.

The great Moses had to learn that the shepherd of God's flock ruled by the crook, and he was sent to Midian for a span of forty years to meditate upon the desert flock, to tame impatience, and to learn to care for the helpless and lead the foolish. When the prince of Egypt burst out again long years later, as we have seen in volume 2 study 82 and Moses beat the rock royally with his staff, he was set aside for leadership and superseded by another.

*7 : The False Shepherds

John 10.1; Matthew 25.31–33; Ezekiel 34.11–19

Wherever good stands there arises the counterfeit. There are, as history, and, alas, everyday experience show, false shepherds. Milton describes them in *Lycidas*:

> *Anow of such as for their bellies' sake,*
> *Creep and intrude, and climb into the fold!*
> *Of other care they little reck'ning make,*
> *Than how to scramble at the shearers' feast,*
> *And shove away the worthy bidden guest;*
> *Blind mouths!*

John Ruskin comments perceptively on this passage. Creep, intrude, climb? 'Do not think,' says Ruskin, 'that Milton uses those three words to fill up his verse. . . . He needs all three, for they exhaustively comprehend the three classes of men who dishonestly seek ecclesiastical power.'

He elaborates: those who 'creep' are those 'who do not care for office, but do all things occultly and cunningly, consenting to any servility of office or conduct so only that they may intimately discern, and unawares direct, the minds of men.' Those who 'intrude', are those 'who by natural insolence of heart and stout eloquence of tongue, and perseverant self-assertion obtain hearing and authority with the common crowd.' Those who 'climb' are those 'who by labour of learning, selfishly exerted in the case of their own ambition, gain high dignities.'

Here is dual exegesis of the first order—John Milton on John 10, and John Ruskin on John Milton. Read on, for this is quota-

19

tion with a purpose: 'Blind mouths.' It is not a broken metaphor. 'The two monosyllables express the contraries of character in two great offices, those of bishop and of pastor.'

A bishop, an 'episkopos' is one who 'oversees'. A pastor is literally 'one who feeds'. The most unbishoply 'overseer' is a bishop who is blind. The most unpastoral character is that of one who, instead of feeding, wishes to be fed. Or turn to Ezek. 34.17–19 and catch the reality of Eastern and Mediterranean history behind the imagery.

The passage, its ellipses supplied, runs: 'Is it a small thing to you goats to have eaten up the good pasture, but you must tread down with your feet the residue? And to have drunk of the deep waters, but you must foul the rest with your feet? A small thing that my sheep must eat what you goats have trampled, and drink what you have fouled with your feet?' The shepherd has also his goats, and separates them when he will. Hence the Lord's own word-picture of the judgement. Like the wheat and the tares the day will separate the true from the false.

8 : Martha and Mary

Luke 10.38–42; John 11.1–5

John has something interesting to say about the Bethany sisters in his Gospel, and we have been following John in recent studies to keep coherence of reading, rather than strict sequence of time. We must return to Luke, however, for the sake of completeness in the story. 'A woman named Martha,' the story runs, idiomatically translated, 'received him into her house. And her sister Mary sat at Jesus' feet, and was listening to his word. Martha, distracted with much serving, came and stood over them and said, "Master, do you not care that my sister has left me alone to serve? Tell her now to take a hand with me." Jesus replied, "Martha, Martha, you are troubled and upset over many things. One thing you need. And that good part Mary has chosen, and it shall not be taken away from her." ' So runs the story. The 'good part' was perhaps a reference to such banqueting customs as we find in Gen. 43.34. Martha is not blamed, but gently shown that the service which distracts and frays the temper is not to be preferred to quiet meditation. Unruffled attention to what the Master has to say leads to truest service. The rush of business, however laudable in motive, can, on the other hand, destroy the spirit's calm, and so mar our spirituality that the service itself loses its effectiveness. Mary had realized that 'man lives not by bread alone', and there is no truth more essential. Without this 'good part' the feast of life loses its spiritual vitamin. The service begins 'at the feet of Jesus'. And so the story becomes a parable of Christian usefulness.

It is interesting to turn to John and observe that it is Martha who is specifically named in v. 5. Does this suggest a preference for Martha? No. He rated differently the service of the two sisters, and Mary on one occasion won the greater share of His approval, but nowhere in the record can we find in Christ that weakness which determines all our human likes and dislikes. 'He knew what was in man,' says John. We do not. Hence our prejudices, our misunderstandings, our hero-worship and irrational affections. He knows us, knows our faults, and loves us equally. Even the phrase 'the disciple whom Jesus loved' implies no lower ranking for his fellows. John's quick apprehension and spiritual insight reached closer to Jesus' heart and won him the favour which love and faith can win, and it was on this basis that the Lord chose the inner circle of His fellowship. There are no degrees in the 'everlasting love'. There are differences in our reception of it. Consider the quiet affection of the Lord's reply to Martha, and consider a very significant phrase in the last Gospel to be written. John was an old man when he closed the canon of the New Testament with his Gospel. He had doubtless heard much misunderstanding of the incident we have considered. And so when his story came to Bethany he wrote with some deliberation the words, 'Now Jesus loved Martha, and her sister, and Lazarus.'

9 : The Bethany Family

John 11.6–46; 12.1–9

It is interesting to watch the characters in the story a little further. Note that it is Martha who is in greater command of the tragic situation (20). Mary, numb with grief, remains in the house, while her sister goes out to meet the Lord. In v. 31 it is Mary who is mentioned as the chief recipient of consolation from the circle of their acquaintance in Jerusalem. It is in such touches of detail that we find the unconscious marks of authenticity. Observe the convincing consistency of characterization.

It is curious that the chief character in the story remains elusive. It is difficult to assess a personality when no reaction in word or deed is recorded. Lazarus says nothing. The only act mentioned is the awesome movement of obedience by which, his arms and legs still wrapped round with the linen bands of death, he emerged from the tomb.

And yet there is one pointer to the sort of person Lazarus was. Jesus wept over his fate, though He knew well what He intended to do. The fact stands in sharp rebuke for those who see virtue in forced joy and cultivated stoicism in the place of death. Jesus wept and groaned in spirit (33, 35). The expression is a strong and vivid one. It is true, as the hymn puts it, that 'there is no love like the love of Jesus', but we are free to guess that it must have been a choice personality who could thus command affection.

Perhaps he was a quiet and placid man, a little overwhelmed by the dynamic Martha, and sharing more closely the contemplative ways of Mary. And his silence leaves us with the vast curiosity unresolved. What happened in those days of death? Had he a memory of any experience? Returned to life, had his values changed? Was he nostalgic for another world? Did he ever again fear death? He was to hold a rare distinction. He shared resurrection with Christ. And so shall we, else 'earth were darkness to the core, and dust and ashes all that is.'

10 : Caiaphas

John 11.47–57; Acts 4.1–22

Caiaphas, in this tiny picture of the doings among the hierarchs, is a repulsive picture. The portrait, for all the few strokes in the composition, is clear enough. This was a frightened man. He had staked all on collaboration with the Romans, and all was life itself. As a Sadducee he had no hope of another life, or for anything beyond such goods as this life might give. He was not prepared to forgo the small accumulation which his planning, intrigue and dissimulation had managed to scrape together, at the hands of a dangerous dreamer, and a reckless mob of enthusiasts.

He was like the political priest of all time, the Grey Eminence

22

who manipulates events, the Wolsey unable to cast away ambition, the Richelieu, the plotting ecclesiastic ready to cloak crime with a crimson robe, and conceal iniquity underneath a mitre. History has no more cynical villains.

Observe the man's rough discourtesy to his peers, and imagine what mercy lesser men might be likely to expect at hands so ruthless and so rough. The Sadducees had something of a reputation for rudeness, and Caiaphas is a notable example.

And note the appeal to expediency. Expediency is the cynical resort and refuge of the hardened in sin of all the ages. Such men have murdered conscience. They have lost their fear of God and of judgement by long practice in self-seeking. They have passed the point of no returning, of which the Lord spoke when He told of a sin beyond all forgiving. Let a man die, innocent or not, said the scoundrel, to save the whole people.

Had that been a sincere word, it would still have stood as inexcusable wrong. Nations founder when principles die. Peoples are lost by abandoning righteousness, even when one life only is at stake. But Caiaphas cared nothing for the nation—'the accursed multitude that knew not the Law' (John 7.49). He was concerned rather for himself, his comfort, and his caste, and it was for that reason that he was willing to murder an innocent man.

There is nothing to redeem Caiaphas. Such creatures, large and small as man measures such matters, are the curse of history, the foes of goodness, the enemies of light. Judgement dogs their steps. It is grim irony that Caiaphas' words contained a meaning beyond his intentions.

11 : The Secret Disciples

John 12.42–50; 1 John 4.2–15; Matthew 10.32, 33

Conviction which produces no action is sterile. Nicodemus is not included in this group. He had, falteringly, made a confession, ineffective though it was. Along with Joseph of Arimathea, his conviction was to force him into the open on a yet more notable occasion.

The unknown men of whom John writes so strongly, won no salvation. The alternatives were stark—the praise of men or the praise of God?—the synagogue or Christ? Visibly before us they make their fatal choice. Westcott is scathing in his comment on this passage: 'Such ineffective, intellectual faith is really the climax of unbelief.'

A heavy burden, indeed, lay upon these men because of their very enlightenment. They knew without doubt where the path of duty lay, but did not take it. They were unwilling to pay the price. The price was popularity and standing in the community, all those advantages, real or imagined, which Paul counted loss for Christ. 'Seek not the favour of the multitude,' said Kant, 'it is seldom got by honest or lawful means. Seek the testimony of the few. Number not voices but weigh them.'

There is no call to court persecution. It is perhaps possible for a devout Christian to be popular, but not likely that his popularity will be permanent. The open avowal of Christ is so frequently the occasion for the world's dislike, that a Christian should examine himself if he finds universal acceptance and approval. It is possible that he has bought the advantage by compromise.

Discipleship cannot be hid, and those who sought to do so were naïve. Discipleship, on the other hand, is not called upon to be brash, tactless, noisy, crude, or in any way to court the world's hostility. Testimony is varied, and is given in a hundred ways. Where the word of the lips might be inappropriate or out of place, the attitude of the person, the manner of his living, the cast of his character in a thousand common and unavoidable situations, will show the committal of the life.

We cannot serve Christ and live a lie, and that is what the men who believed among the rulers sought to do. They began with foundations. They could not remain at that immobile point. They either lapsed into open sin or moved on to open discipleship.

Questions and themes for study and discussion on Studies 6–11

1. The kind of spiritual leadership represented by the shepherd image.
2. The marks of a true and of a false shepherd of God's flock.
3. Martha and proper hospitality.
4. The true balance of Christian activity and personal devotion.
5. Is expediency ever a correct guide to a proper course of action?
6. 'Secret discipleship' as a contradiction in terms.

LIFE IN CHRIST

The Pattern Life

12 : The Ten Commandments

Exodus 20.1–17

Whether the Ten Commandments are as familiar as they used to be, or ought to be, is doubtful; but it is possible to know them by heart and still miss much of their meaning, as did the Pharisees in our Lord's day. Note the following points.

1. God gave the commandments to Israel in His character as Yahweh, their God and Redeemer (2). Loyalty to their Lord, and gratitude for His work of grace, were to be the motive of their obedience. They were given the law, not to show them how to earn God's favour and acceptance (they had that already), but to guide them in living the life that would please Him, and bring them the fullness of His blessing (6, 12).

2. Though nine commandments are stated negatively, thus focusing on the points at which lawlessness starts (always a good way of inculcating moral alertness!), positive principles are implied, thus: give your God total loyalty; in all your dealings with Him, think of Him only as He has revealed Himself, and not in any other terms; always be reverent; use your weekly day of rest to worship your Maker and Redeemer (cf. v. 11 with Deut. 5.15), and to help others (Mark 3.2 ff.); respect and love your fellow men, and seek their welfare; respect the sanctity of marriage-vows and the integrity of the opposite sex; respect property; stay truthful and straight; be content with what God has given you. Law-keeping was always a matter, not just of avoiding irreligious and anti-social actions in public, but of loving service to God (6, Deut. 6.5) and one's neighbour (Lev. 19.18).

3. Though stated in terms of outward action, the commandments touch the heart, calling for right desires and attitudes (cf. Jesus' exposition of the sixth and seventh commandments, Matt. 5.21–30).

The commandments were given as God's covenant requirement of Israel, but the principles embodied in them go back to

25

creation, and what they are pointing to is the shape of the ideal life, not just for Israelites, but for man as such. Law-keeping, which is what God's image and likeness involves (cf. Gen. 1.26; Eph. 4.24), is what human nature was made for, and there is no true human fulfilment, just as there is no true godliness, without it.

For an exposition of the Ten Commandments, questions 99 to 148 of the Westminster Larger Catechism, and *The Ten Commandments*, by Thomas Watson (Banner of Truth), are recommended.

13 : Portrait of a Happy Man

Matthew 5.1–12

The Kingdom of God is the reign of Christ over converted sinners, and the Sermon on the Mount is its charter: a discourse for disciples (1 f.), showing in ideal form how citizens of the Kingdom will live, and how God will bless and use them. Controlling the whole Sermon is the thought that God is the Father, and as such the guardian and rewarder, of Jesus' disciples (9; 6.4, 6, 8–15, 18, 26–32; 7.11). The blessings of the beatitudes should be understood as the Father's ways of enriching His children, now and hereafter. 'The kingdom of heaven' in vs. 3, 10 means the family relationship with God through Christ, together with all that flows from it, and the promises of the other beatitudes are of particular 'kingdom blessings' from our Heavenly Father's store.

The nine beatitudes are a series of promises, and those who qualify for the promised gift are spoken of each time as 'blessed'. The Greek word does not mean 'object of blessing', as the English reader might suppose; it means *happy, fortunate, enjoying an enviable lot*. This is paradoxical, for the qualifications include conscious inner poverty (3), mourning (4), dissatisfaction with one's own state (6), and being an object of hatred and ill-treatment (10 f.). But the principles of life in the Kingdom, according to the Sermon, are grace and faith—the free giving of God 'to enrich the humble poor', and the disciple's trust and confidence in God the giver (cf. the definition of faith in Heb. 11.1). It is what God gives to the disciple, not what he has in himself, that makes his lot happy.

26

The qualities of the happy man may be summarized thus: his sense of inner poverty (3) comes from knowledge of his sinfulness, his mourning (4) from desire to be rid of it, and his craving for righteousness (6) from a passion to please God. He is meek (5) in that he does not assert himself, and when others exploit, abuse and maltreat him because of his Christian stand (10 f.) he quietly accepts it, as from God, not seeking revenge but continuing gentle and loving towards them (see this in Jesus, Matt. 11.29 and 1 Pet. 2.23; and in Moses, Num. 12.3 and the whole chapter). His mercifulness to those who do not deserve mercy (7), and his passion for peacemaking (9), are aspects of his meekness and of his Christlikeness (cf. Heb. 2.17 f.; Mark 9.50; Eph. 2.14). His purity of heart relates not only to the seventh commandment (27 ff.) but to his single-minded determination to seek and serve God in everything rather than indulge himself (cf. 6.19–24). All these qualities, apart from the sense of sin, are seen supremely in Jesus Himself, and the reward promised in each case shows how God delights in them.

14 : An Example

John 13.1–20

Jesus' washing of His disciples' feet during the Last Supper (4) was an acted parable of spiritual cleansing, and thus a token of redeeming love (1, 7–10). As told there, the episode reveals three aspects of His glory:

1. *Jesus' Divine Knowledge.* As Son of God, He knew He would soon return to His Father to reign (1, 3); as Searcher of hearts (cf. 2.25), He knew which of His chosen disciples were 'clean' (i.e. forgiven and accepted by God) and which one was not 'clean' and would betray Him (10 f., 18 f.). Also, He knew that His road back to the Father led through the ultimate humiliation of the cross, the humiliation which He symbolized here by taking the role of a low-grade menial. There is no support here for the idea, canvassed by some, that the conditions of the incarnation limited Jesus' knowledge.

2. *Jesus' Saving Love.* He loved His own 'to the *end*'—that is, according to John's habit of multiple meaning, to the end of His earthly life and of His redemptive work, and also to the last degree. A Jewish host normally had his guests' feet washed by

an underling; Jesus, as host at the Supper, does the job Himself, first taking off His coat to reveal Himself as a true Servant in action (4 f.). A modern equivalent of feet-washing would be shoe-cleaning. The initiative, as always, was with Jesus. Simon Peter disapproved of Jesus thus demeaning Himself and, Simonlike, said so (cf. Matt. 16.22 f.). Jesus' words in v. 8, however, made him change his tune, and instead of refusing to have his feet washed he asked for total immersion! Jesus' reply (10) showed that daily cleansing within an already established relation of acceptance was the particular blessing which the feetwashing signified.

3. *Jesus' Divine Authority.* As Teacher, Lord, and Director of His disciples' lives, He charges them to follow His example of loving service. The particular service which the feet-washing signified was unique (i.e., cleansing from sin), but the spirit of love and care which the action revealed is not to be unique: Christians must reproduce it. It is in the first instance by maintaining an attitude of self-humbling love, rather than by particular outward behaviour-patterns, that Christians are called upon to imitate Christ (cf. Eph. 5.1 f.).

15 : The Greatest Thing

1 Corinthians 13

The Greek word *agape* (love) seems to have been virtually a Christian invention, a new word for a new thing (apart from about twenty occurrences in the Greek version of the O.T., it is almost non-existent before the N.T.). For *agape* draws its meaning directly from the revelation of God in Christ. *Agape* is not a form of natural affection, however intense, but a supernatural fruit of the Spirit (Gal. 5.22). It is a matter of will rather than of feeling (for Christians must love even those whom they dislike: Matt. 5.44–48). It is the basic element in Christlikeness. Christian love is '*Calvary* love'. Paul here hymns love as the greatest thing in the world (cf. v. 13), and the 'still more excellent way' (12.31, cf. 14.1) for those who would find God's best.

1. *The Primacy of Love* (1–3). Tongues, prophetic gifts, theological expertise and miracle-working faith (1 f., cf. 12.9 f.; Mark 11.22 f.), all true gifts of God in the apostolic age, preoccupied the Corinthians; giving everything away and accepting

martyrdom (cf. Mark **10**.22; Luke **12**.33; Matt. **10**.21 f.) may be required of Christians at any time. Yet love matters so much more than these things that without it they all become worthless, and the loveless Christian, however gifted and active, gains nothing and is nothing (i.e. his works will perish, to his shame and loss: 3.10–15). Paul wants the Corinthians to see that the grace of a loving heart is better than any amount of ability and loveless labour.

2. *The Profile of Love* (4–7). These statements about love make up a portrait of Jesus; from this standpoint the four Gospels are the best commentary on them. Also, they comprehensively correct the bumptious, contentious, suspicious, presumptuous, arrogant, self-assertive, critical, irresponsible spirit because of which Paul had to call the Corinthians carnal, and spiritually babyish (3.1; cf. **1**.11. f., **3**.3; **4**.6 f., 18; **5**.2, 6; **6**.8; **8**.1–3; **9**.3; **10**.6–13; **11**.17–22). Love neither condones others' sins (6) nor is hostile, cynical, or exploiting, but is absorbed in seeking others' good.

3. *The Permanence of Love* (8–13). The greater importance of love appears from the fact that it will last through the life to come, when all occasion for tongues, prophecy and theological instruction will have ceased.

16 : Hope and Holiness

1 Peter 1.13–21

Applied to God (the fundamental usage) the word 'holy' signifies everything about Him that sets Him apart from men; notably, His power and purity. Applied to men, the word signifies, first, the relation of being consecrated to God's service and use, and accepted for it, and secondly, the quality of Godlikeness which one displays in one's living. Holiness of life involves both *worship*, in which God's truth draws us out into responsive praise and prayer, and *obedience*, whereby we fulfil the patterns set for us in God's law (cf. **2**.9). These are the ideas expressed in the directive of Lev. **11**.44 f. and (quoting Leviticus) vs. 15 f.: 'you (my people) shall be holy, for I (your God) am holy.'

Verses 13 f. work up to this summons. Verse 13 is a warning against three evils which blight the Christian life. The first is being *slack*—so 'gird up your minds', pull yourselves together—

concentrate! The second is being *haphazard*, the way of the drunkard—so 'be sober'—discipline yourself, be purposeful and alert! The third is being *double-minded*, the evil that results from looking too hard at the world's present attractions and not hard enough at the prospects held out to us by God's promises— so 'hope *fully*', *fix* your hope on what is to come. Holy living is powerfully motivated by the hope of glory with Christ (cf. v. 21; 1 John 3.2 f.). To Christians who, like Peter's readers, and like Christians living under hostile regimes today, face hardship and ill-treatment for Christ's sake for the remainder of their stay on earth (cf. 4.12–19), such a hope is supremely stabilizing and encouraging (cf. Rom. 8.24 f.). (RSV's 'exile' in v. 17 is a mistranslation: Peter's point is not that they are for the present barred out of Heaven, but simply that this world is only a temporary place of residence, and not their real home.)

Over and above the power of hope, Peter invokes two more motives for holy living. The first is their sense of privilege (18–21), springing from knowledge of three things: first, the *preciousness* of the blood of Christ which was shed for them; second, the *concern* God has shown for their redemption, designating His Son for this task before ever they existed; third, their *adoption* as God's sons and heirs through the new birth (14, 17). The second motive is their sense of reverence for the God who is related to them as a just Judge as well as a loving Father (17). This filial reverence (not panic and terror) is the meaning of the 'fear' of God (17, cf. Psa. 111.10; Prov. 1.7, 29; Acts 9.31).

17: In His Steps

1 Peter 2.18–25

Christians today, like slaves in Peter's day (18), are often in jobs and relationships where they are not fairly treated, but are made to suffer wrongfully. Now as then, however, there is support for such sufferers in the gospel—support which will make possible the patient endurance (19) which God requires. 'Mindful of God' (19, RSV) is a poor translation: the Greek means 'for the sake of (i.e. in deference to) a God-informed conscience', and points to the Christian's knowledge that he is called to a life of innocent suffering, after Christ's example (21). 'The heirs of salvation, I know from His word, through much tribulation must follow their Lord' (John Newton, cf. Acts 14.22).

This is one of many places in the New Testament where a magnificent statement of doctrine slips in quite incidentally to make an ethical point. Verses 22–25 are a rich though compressed review of God's plan of salvation. Peter dwells on Christ's role as God's suffering servant, in language that echoes Isa. 53. He calls attention to Jesus' total innocence (22), and His patience under provocation and pain (23, cf. Matt. 27.12–14; John 19. 8–11). He then explains that His innocent suffering was actually a work of vicarious sin-bearing (24, cf. v. 21; 3.18); he reminds them that God purposed through this to bring them into a new life, in which they said good-bye to sin and lived henceforth by God's law (24, cf. 4.1 f.); and finally he brings before them the fact that they have already turned from their life of sinful wanderings to the living Christ (God's vindication of Jesus through resurrection and exaltation is assumed, though not mentioned), so that Christ has now become their Shepherd and Overseer—that is, leader and protector (25). 'Overseer' is *episkopos*—'Guardian' in the RSV, 'Bishop' in the AV (KJV)—and the phrase reminds us that the pastoral oversight exercised by Christian ministers must always reflect and subserve the perpetual pastorate of Christ Himself.

What Peter wants his readers to learn from all this is that to follow in the steps of our Saviour through suffering is in fact an honour for us (cf. Phil. 1.29)—just as it is something which delights God and wins His approval. Following Christ's example in the New Testament means two things: loving and serving others (as in John 13.1–20, cf. Study 14) and enduring maltreatment while one does so (as here).

Questions and themes for study and discussion on Studies 12–17

1. What place should the ten commandments take in the modern world?
2. What are the links between faith, hope and love in Christian discipleship?
3. Is law-keeping an adequate description of Christian obedience? If not, what needs to be added?
4. In what ways are Christians called to imitate Christ?
5. Murray McCheyne prayed: 'Lord, make me as holy as it is possible for a saved sinner to be.' What would an answer to this prayer involve?
6. Work out in detail what it means to be humble and meek.

CHARACTER STUDIES

18 : Peter

Matthew 14.22–36; Mark 6.45–56

Here is something curious. Matthew tells of Peter's characteristic over-confidence, and his failure on the water. It was typical of the rash disciple to act on a gust of emotion and to underestimate his capabilities. But why does Mark, who drew his facts from Peter, omit the incident? There is no ready explanation. Peter was not a man to suppress any matter which did not reflect well upon himself. That is more than once demonstrated in Mark's narrative. Nor had he anything of which to be ashamed. 'Beginning to sink', he cried for help to the only available source, and received it. There is nothing else to do when there is nothing solid underneath the feet. We must leave Mark's brevity unexplained. On the other hand there are some familiar marks of Peter's presence behind the words of the story. Perhaps there is an echo of the blunt words of Peter in v. 52. This, in fact, may be the point Peter stressed for Mark, and so determined the character of his narrative. It is the way of men to require repeated assurance; Gideon asked for the double sign of the dew and the fleece. And it is the fashion of the heart to forget the boon received and the mercy given, to doubt the wonder of it, and imagine that, after all, some astounding chance or unusual circumstance produced a seeming miracle. In our dealings with God there is always this margin of uncertainty, for God thrusts His presence on no man; He reveals Himself to faith and not to sight. That is why He tested His men immediately after the miracle on the hillside. On the earlier occasion of storm on the lake, He had been with them in the ship. Now He withdraws, as though to teach them to battle alone and to rely upon an aid they could not see; He sends them into the tumult and darkness without His visible presence. God often does this. It is His will that we should grow to spiritual maturity, and trust where we cannot see. Too often in such situations of testing, past lessons are forgotten, and fear banishes faith. But God is always in the shadows, keeping watch over His own. We have only to cry out and He is by our side.

19 : The Pharisees Again

Mark 7.1–23

As we resume the tenuous thread of narrative from Mark, we meet the Pharisees once more. Again one can almost hear the blunt words of Peter behind the account, and the niggling, hostile custodians of formal Judaism appear again in firm portraiture before us, eager to preserve the petty observances and sophistries of their elaborate code, but blind, as Isaiah put it, to the realities of life, and to the enormous obligations of mercy and duty.

Such is human nature that it is much easier to obey a set of rules and to call that obedience righteousness, than to live unselfishly and daily to seek the will and pleasure of the Lord. The Pharisees are a sad sight. They began as a great people, and to them, as we have seen, goes the credit for purging Israel of idolatry and establishing that reverence for the law and word of God which was Judaism's great contribution to the world. But the nature of man is such that great movements and institutions seldom escape ultimate corruption. God uses and discards—and discard He must, when that which began in purity ends in self-seeking and pride . . .

> The old order changeth, yielding place to new,
> And God fulfils Himself in many ways . . .

In meticulous observance of their own interpretation of the law, the Pharisees forgot mercy and loving-kindness. In jealous watching for infringements of their petty taboos, they failed to see the glory of God in Christ. Nor is such a pernicious attitude limited to the ancient Pharisee. Christianity has its ethics and observances, but it is the never-ending fault of man to reduce its grand obligations to formal codes, with their exits and their entrances; to set form above the spirit, to condition salvation beyond the Lord's intent, and, commonest fault of all, to resurrect the old Pharisaic interpretation of a Chosen People set apart from lesser men.

We shall meet the Pharisees again. Blind in their pride and folly, they were blundering on to the great crime which has darkened their memory—the alliance with the worldly Sadducees and the murder of Christ.

20 : The Woman of Tyre

Mark 7.24–37; Isaiah 23.1–12

This was the Lord's furthest journey north. It was the only occasion on which He left the proper territory of Israel. A track leads over the hills from Galilee, cut today by a hostile frontier, and to the astonishment of His men the Lord led that way, down to the ancient city of Tyre, once a seat of maritime empire. One might imagine that He knew of one in need there. In the wide ruins of Tyre a street paved in mosaic is uncovered. It is a first-century street, once a shopping mall, with geometrical designs in the paving and columns on each side. At the street's western end the Mediterranean glitters over the ruins of ancient port facilities.

Here they met the clever Phoenician and a strange conversation took place amid the circle of the disciples standing disapprovingly round. There was no harshness in the Lord's reply to the woman of Tyre. It is obvious that there must be a background not detailed in the narrative. The territory was populated by remnants of the Canaanites, and was sure to stir the racial consciousness of the disciples. The conversation all morning as they entered Gentile territory may have been in scorn of the foreigner —'these dogs'. In sad irony the Lord speaks rather to His protesting companions than to the needy woman. With quick wit she catches His meaning and replies in the same spirit, but in a humble tone which wins commendation and reward.

His healing, indeed, was for the world. Even in alien Phoenicia, as v. 24 puts it, 'He could not be hid.' Christ cannot be concealed. Secret discipleship is not discipleship at all. We have already discussed that truth. A home must be different where He truly resides. A character which owns His lordship must reveal its allegiance. A life which seeks His will, however haltingly, cannot disguise the fact. A Christian's path and the world's do not coincide. Situations arise which call for confession in word or deed, in protest or abstention. We must accept the truth that our allegiance cannot be hid, and seek to make life, speech, and attitude, a worthy testimony to our Lord—quiet, gracious, tactful, free from arrogance, from all suspicion of self-righteousness, and, above all, from inconsistency.

21 : Peter's Confession

Matthew 16.13–20; Mark 8.27–38

The strange words of Matt. 16.19 do not mean that Peter was given special authority over the destinies of men. Peter was recognized, by these words, as possessing didactic, not judicial, authority. An interpretation must be true to its context. Take the former. Peter has shown a God-given insight into truth which has delighted his Master. He has grasped a doctrine fundamental to Christian faith. It seems natural, then, that any authority he may be granted in reward should have reference to doctrine rather than to administration. Then think of the psychological context, the imagery, in other words. In English the metaphor in the word 'key' is coloured by Roman law, by feudalism, and medieval keeps. A word can suggest vastly different ideas in different lands and ages. The 'key' in the Lord's word here quoted had reference to the schools of the scribes. A proficient scribe was said to be in possession of the keys of the Law. Peter, as it were, graduates. So keen has been his apprehension of truth that he can be trusted to unlock the expressions of Heaven, to loosen the bonds of unsanctified doctrine, to confirm the constraints of Heaven's behests. This interpretation is not upset by the use of the key as a symbol of authority in Revelation. The two contexts support each other. Peter's authority was that of the school, not the court-house.

Turn then to Mark's account. Mark's brevity draws closely together in the story Peter's confession and Peter's mistake. From Matthew's account it is clear that some time lay between. Nor does Mark mention the word of splendid tribute to Peter. It is easy to see why, if Peter was Mark's chief source of information. One can imagine the brevity with which that great spirit would pass over the record of commendation, or even bid that no mention be made of it. The deep humility, born of the tragic denial in the high priest's house, would similarly prompt frankness for the record of mistakes. Out of his failure Peter was eager to pluck good. Failure, equally with success (if completely surrendered to the transforming hands of God), can be used for the blessing of men. Many a bruised, defeated man, remembering Peter, has risen from defeat and battled on. Had Peter suppressed the story of his fall, or hidden the words of the Lord's rebuke, there would have been failure unhealed in all the centuries and defeat unremedied. Peter's faults, handed in penitence and helplessness to God, were transfigured by the Hands which can turn all things to good.

22 : On The Transfiguration Mount

Mark 9.2–13; 1 Kings 12.12–16

The pattern of worth and failure is seen throughout Peter's story. He is selected by his Master as one of the privileged group which was to see His Transfiguration; it is part of the love of God to measure us by our desires for good rather than by our achievement, and Peter's intent was true. If the favour of God and the blessing He bestows depended upon our understanding of His purposes, our lot would be hopeless indeed. The meaning of the awesome scene on the mountain still eludes us. It is recorded as an amazing experience of three bewildered men, and Peter's reaction was in conformity with his character. In moments of tension or emotion he took refuge in speech, and often his hasty words were ill-advised. We have seen him earn rebuke. On the mount he makes a wild suggestion which may mean the setting up of a standard of revolt. Was this 'seeing the Kingdom of God coming with power'? Peter may well have asked himself. Peter was afraid, and speaking excitedly, when he suggested the setting up of the three tents, 'one for you and one for Moses and one for Elijah,' but, as people do under such circumstances, he was revealing his inner thoughts. 'To your tents, O Israel,' (1 Kings 12.16) was a rallying cry for Jewish rebels. Peter believed perhaps that the Lord was about to 'manifest Himself', as the conquering Messiah, and he made his suggestion in that light. His confused mind pictured Jews streaming to the wilderness, armed for final battle with the Roman, and rallying under three standards, those of Jesus, Moses and Elijah! Little wonder the apostles proved so spiritually impotent the very next day! And we may imagine the disappointment of their Lord. They quarrelled over precedence in the Kingdom on the last journey to Jerusalem. Two of them, walking to Emmaus, revealed that they had held a narrow nationalism to the end of their relations with the Lord. And now Peter fails to grasp the wonder of his Master on the Transfiguration Mount. The Lord was ever under the necessity of avoiding enthusiastic crowds, lest they 'make Him King'. Too many false Messiahs arose, too many tents were 'set up' in the desert only to be mopped up by Roman flying columns. Peter's project is passed by in silence, and with that gentle suppression with which God seems so often to quench our feverish scheming. It found no condemnation, for the motive was pure.

23 : The Disciples

Mark 9.14–32; Psalm 9

The three, with their Master, came down from Hermon. A considerable crowd awaited them, 'a great crowd', Mark says, with some intermingling of doctors-of-the-law from Caesarea Philippi. It is difficult to account for such a popular demonstration unless some unwise boasting or courting of popularity on the part of the disciples is the reason for it.

The centre of interest was a stricken man in agony of mind over his son. He had come to seek Christ's help for the afflicted lad, who was torn and tormented by an evil thing which possessed him. There is no greater pain than the helpless anguish of a parent who would gladly bear the burden of a child's woe, but can only watch and grieve.

The man came seeking Christ and found His followers. Men still come in fear and in yearning to seek the assurance and the hope He has to give and find too often the preacher without conviction, or the Christian without a message. Let all who diminish Christ, make God remote, too little, the servant of a sect, or anything less than the Lord Omnipotent get out of the way. There is more in the story than Mark's brief narrative tells. Peter, after all, was not at first present, and Peter was Mark's authority. The story is full enough from the point of his arrival. The nine disciples were riding a wave of popular interest. It is easy enough to collect a crowd. Pathetic stunting in the Church often succeeds well enough in this trivial process. But to what end?

Note, too, that the scribes were there. The doctors of the law were interested in the prophet from Galilee and His men, and the disciples were not a little proud, and anxious to turn the situation to profit. Perhaps in their innocence they were out to impress the religious leaders with a notable miracle. But as the great James Denney once remarked: 'No one can bear witness to himself and Jesus Christ at one and the same time. No man can at one and the same time show that he himself is clever and that Christ is mighty to save.' 'Here now, you rebels,' shouted Moses, 'shall

37

we bring forth water for you out of this rock?' It was disaster in his great career.

A man-made mass-movement is harmful. The exaltation of a person or an institution in empty religious excitement is lamentable. Christ is hidden, the way barred to His healing hand, when strutting self-important men advertise their sham religious wares before the multitude. Christ can work only through the humble, the devoted, the dependent. He chooses 'the weak things of the world' to do His work. The man who said those words was one of the most powerful intellects of his age, and God chose Saul of Tarsus because he wished to use the sharp clean tool of his great mind. But that mind had to be surrendered, conscious of its need, malleable in His hand . . .

*24 : The Parent

Mark 9.14–32; Luke 11.11–13

We have set down the passage from Mark for a second reading, for we now shift the emphasis from the disciples to the father.

'Bring the boy to me,' said Christ, and there in five words is the divine commission for parents and teachers. It is an awful thought that we are the child's first image of God.

'Bring the boy to me,' said Christ, and we ourselves dare not approach that Presence unworthily. How humbly must we tread when we lead a child by the hand!

And so they brought the child to Christ. There is a note of hopelessness in the distracted father's voice: 'I asked your disciples to cast him out but they could not.' It is possible to catch the dull, flat tone of a disillusioned man. The chill of impotence of those who should have aided him is on his heart even in the presence of the Lord: 'But *if you* can do anything', he says without much hope, 'have pity on us and help us.'

The Lord looked at him and said: 'If *you* can! All things are possible to one who believes.' At the words the man's heart caught fire. In days of doubt we should look steadily on His face. Turn the eyes on Him, and the world grows dim, the clutter of humanity falls away, and the heart grows strong. 'Lord,' he cried, 'I believe. Help my unbelief.' So the AV (KJV) and Moffatt. 'I do believe. Help me to believe more,' says J. B. Phillips. 'I have faith. Help me where faith falls short,' runs the New English

38

Bible. Or translate: 'I believe, I believe, pity my faith's feebleness.'

So cried the poor man, and put a magnificent prayer into history. It is a prayer which, of all prayers, can claim an answer. The Lord demands no impossible coercion of mind or soul. He presents no list of man-made dogmas. He asks for no intellectual dishonesty, no vain words, or insincere profession. He asks us to look steadily in His eyes, and trust Him to be what He professed to be. He asks for a willingness to try, for the merest bridgehead in the soul. None can help the surge of doubt, but doubt need not be fostered and cherished, misnamed integrity of mind, and laced with pride and posturing.

A burning desire for God must lie at the core of all faith. Perhaps in the mystery of God's ways with men, that is why faith saves. Doubt too often finds its origin in a half-suppressed desire *not* to believe, to find some way out of faith's stern obligations. The father in the story wanted blessing, and with that firm invincible desire beneath its feet faith found a place to kneel and then to stand.

*25 : The Child

Mark 9.25–29; Matthew 18.1–10

There is an unnamed person in the crowd which the Lord joined with His selected disciples—silent save for the cries of an afflicted child. A small figure leaves the scene quietened and healed, but he stands for the multitude of children to whom Christ has brought love, peace and manifold compassion.

The life of children was of small account in the ancient world, and it is a significant mark of those sections of society which abandon Christ today, that the tenderness which comes with Christian parenthood fails and falters. Unborn life is considered of less and less account in a sex-ridden society. It is a small step to the contempt for newly born life which marked the ancient world, and permitted the casting out of unwanted babes to die on the town's rubbish-heap.

Among the multitude of papyrus letters which have survived from the arid sands south of Cairo, is one written within a year or two of the birth of a Child in Bethlehem. A certain young man had gone north from his native village to find work in the teeming

39

metropolis of Alexandria. His wife had written to him anxiously. She was to have a child in his absence and no doubt enquired concerning her husband's wishes. He writes back with some affection, but casually bids her throw the babe away if it is a girl. Here is the letter. (The date is the year we call 1 B.C.):

'Hilarion to his dear wife Alis, very many greetings, likewise to my lady Berous and Apollonarion. Know that we are still in Alexandria. Do not be anxious; if they really go home, I will remain in Alexandria. I beg and entreat you, take care of the little one, and as soon as we receive our pay I will send it up to you. If by chance you bear a child, if it is a boy, let it be, if it is a girl, cast it out. You have said to Aphrodisias: 'Do not forget me.' How can I forget you? I beg you then not to be anxious. The 29th year of Caesar Augustus, Month of Pauni, 23. Deliver to Alis from Hilarion.'

There is a certain significance, then, in the shaken little boy who walked off with his father to some small home in Caesarea Philippi.

Questions and themes for study and discussion on Studies 18–25

1. 'Beginning to sink' as an experience of life.
2. Pharisaism today.
3. References in the Gospels to Gentiles.
4. How could Peter's faults of too ready speech be turned to good account?
5. How can Christians obscure Christ?
6. You have read material from John and from Mark. How do their styles differ?
7. Human character. Has it changed?
8. 'Christianity is a charter for children.' Discuss this.

LIFE IN CHRIST

Identification with Christ

26 : The Way of the Cross

Mark 8.31–38; Galatians 2.20; 6.11–18

In the first passage, having stated and reaffirmed against Peter the
necessity of His being rejected and executed (31–33), Jesus
declares that anyone who would 'come after' Him (that is, learn
what it means to go His way) must do three things. First, he must
give up all right to himself (34)—that is, cease bothering about
self-preservation (35), self-aggrandizement (36), and self-protec-
tion against ridicule (38), and abandon self-assertion as a way of
life. This is the condition in which 'the world is crucified to me'
(Gal. 6.14). Second, he must take up his cross—that is, settle for
a life into which the world's favour and esteem do not enter.
Only criminals going to execution—men, that is, from whom the
world's favour had been totally withdrawn—carried crosses in
those days (cf. John 19.17). This is the condition in which one is
'crucified to the world' (Gal. 6.14). Third, the would-be disciple
must 'follow' Jesus in the sense of accepting as leader and guide
One who was even then on His way to crucifixion, and who
expected to involve His disciples in sufferings corresponding to
His own (10.39; Matt. 10.25). This, says Jesus, is the only path
that leads to life (35).

In the second passage, having told how he, a Jew, came to see
that the law had not brought him righteousness and life (16, 21;
3.21 f.), but only a necessity of death (19), Paul states that his
acceptance of Christ, and Christ's cross, as his only means of
life with God, had involved accepting the law's death-sentence on
him and regarding himself henceforth as having been 'crucified
with Christ'. My old life, says Paul, has finished—under judgement; now, by faith in the Christ who died for me—the Christ
who now lives for me—I live the new life of self-denial, Christ-
centred, Christ-indwelt, and Christ-controlled, and I find it to be
life indeed. The two aspects of the Christian's identification with
Christ—acceptance of His cross as both the end of one's old life
and the pattern of one's new life—are here brought together.

41

In Gal. 6.11–18, the postscript in Paul's own handwriting (11), Paul insists that true Christianity—that is, 'new creation' (15) and the enjoyment of God's peace and mercy (16)—flows from accepting total solidarity with Christ's cross, embracing it as one's path and passport to life, and making it one's only pride and joy (14).

27 : Risen, Freed, and Enslaved

Romans 6

This great chapter teaches that saving union with Christ by faith brings 'newness of life' (4) through incorporation into Christ's own dying and rising. Christ's person, cross and resurrection, although historically located in Palestine in about A.D. 30 are 'trans-historical' realities. The risen Christ 'fills all things' (Eph. 4.10): every believer everywhere in every age touches Him, lives 'in' Him, and is made new by Him. From co-crucifixion and co-resurrection with Christ flow freedom from sin's dominion (6 f., 14, 16–18), a new enslavement to God and to righteousness (18, 22), the hope of bodily resurrection (5, 8–10), and eternal life as God's free gift (23). There follows also an obligation not to let indwelling sin regain mastery at any point (12–19). You need never give in to sinful urges, says Paul (14), and that is something to thank God for (17), since bondage to sin brings only death (21). Paul's theme here is new creation (cf. 2 Cor. 5.17); his point is that those who are 'under grace' (14 f.) must live differently from before, because in Christ they really are different people.

Particular points to note:

1. Verse 1 means 'Shall we carry on under sin's sway as before?' —to which v. 2 replies that since we are different we can't, and should not dream of trying.

2. Baptism-imagery is used in vs. 3 f. because Christian baptism is a sign of initiation (starting a relationship with Christ), termination (ending one's old life), dedication, and renewal.

3. Sin (6, 12, 14, 16, 18, 20, 22) is an anti-God 'drive', or 'twist' of nature, mastering unbelievers and still indwelling Christians (7.17, 20, 23). Sin will remain with us as long as our bodies are 'mortal' and unrenewed (12, cf. 8.23). This, and not any depreciation of physical nature as such, is the point of Paul's references to the body of 'sin' and 'death' (6.6; 7.24).

4. 'Know' (3, 6, 9, 16), 'believe' (8), 'consider' (11) are key words: for the basis of Christian holiness is taking God's word about the inward change He has effected and then living out what He has wrought in (cf. Phil. 2.12 f.).

5. 'Yield' (13, 16, 19), or 'present', implies consent of will. Paul is calling for a life of repentance and consecration (19, 22, where 'sanctification' means 'consecrated state', cf. 12.1 f.). He is not here discussing the continuing involuntary shortcomings of the consecrated, which he deals with in Rom. 7.14–25; 8.23; Gal. 5.17.

6. It is through faith's obedience to gospel truth that the inward work of grace replacing sin's rule by God's becomes a reality (17).

28 : Holding Fast the Head

Colossians 2.6–19

Verses 6–8 sum up the message of Colossians. Let Jesus Christ be everything to you, says Paul; live (literally 'walk') 'in Him' (6), acknowledging Him as the ground in which you are rooted and the One who builds you up in the Church (cf. v. 19), for whom you should constantly give God thanks (7, cf. 3.17), because of the 'wealth' and 'treasures' He has brought you (1.27; 2.3). And don't be 'conned' by any supposed 'wisdom' from non-Christian sources, whether ordinary 'worldly wisdom' or derived from the occult, into doing anything else (8)! 'Philosophy' here means heretical theosophy; 'the world', 'human tradition', emanates from human society organized without God and banded against God; on the 'elemental spirits' or 'rudiments', see note on study 29.

Paul's directive follows from his doctrine of who and what Christ is. In His own right as God's incarnate Son and Image (1.13–15, 19; 2.9), Maker and Master of the universe and Lord of the Church (1.16–18), and also as the complete answer to our spiritual needs (10) through His atonement for our sins (1.20; 2.13 f.), His indwelling in our hearts (1.27), and the new life with God that He brings (13), Christ is and must be pre-eminent (1.18). Paul piles up imagery, sacramental and secular, to highlight Christ's adequacy. In Christ, he says, God has renewed your hearts (inward circumcision and burial in baptism, vs. 11 f.). Having found you spiritually dead, He brought you to life with Christ through faith (risen in baptism and forgiven, vs. 12 f., cf.

Eph. 2. 1 ff.). Through the cross He cancelled our death sentence which the broken law demanded (14) and overthrew all the forces of cosmic evil. For those who have eyes to see, Christ's cross, which looked like a humiliating defeat, was actually His march of triumph, in which He led His foes captive, in the manner of a Roman general after a successful campaign (15).

Paul's central point is that nobody needs more than Christ gives. For a Christian to turn to Judaizing ritualism (16 f.), angel-worship (18), and the murky world of 'visions' (18), is not gain, but loss. Christ alone makes the Church (His body) live and grow spiritually. Christians must 'hold fast to the Head' (19), and not seek spiritual enrichment from other sources; it is not there to be had, and to seek it is to lose touch with Christ. Paul is attacking the particular errors of the Colossian theosophists, but modern occultism and superstition fall equally under his apostolic ban.

29 : Christ is our Life

Colossians 2.20–3.15

The deepest reason why Christians must accept identification with Christ as the controlling principle for their lives is that God has actually united them with Christ in His dying and rising. When Christ rose, He ascended to God's 'right hand', i.e. a state of glory and dominion in His Father's immediate presence. When Christians are made alive in Christ, they at once enter into this same realm of spiritual realities, transcending space and time, where they have fellowship with the Father and the Son (cf. 1 John 1.3). Christ is henceforth their 'life' in the sense that all their communion with God flows from Him and relates to Him, and will continue so for ever. This 'life' of theirs is hidden so far as the eye of sense is concerned, just as Christ Himself is; but when Christ is manifested in glory at His coming, Christians will be with Him, and His relation to them as their life will then be plain to see (3 f.).

The presupposition of our enjoying this 'life' is that we 'died' with Christ—that is, finished with the world and its ways (20). Whether we died to 'elemental spirits', i.e. bad angels, the 'world-rulers of this present darkness' (Eph. 6.12)—so RSV—or to the 'rudiments' of the world's wisdom—so AV (KJV)—is disputed, but the point is in either case the same. A clean break with the past has been made (death is the cleanest break imaginable). The 'old man' has been put off and the 'new man' put on (3.9 f.; the image is of changing clothes). What goes on now is a new life entirely, a life which the world does not control. This is the situation into which God has brought all who have received Christ; and now we must live it out.

How are we to do that? First, by recognizing that the world's way of religion (such things as legalism, man-made restrictions, holiness equated with abstinence and austerity) is in truth just one more form of self-indulgence which must be given up (20–23). Second, we must recognize that the world's way of behaviour (self-indulgence in immorality; exploiting others in hostility) must be 'put to death' (3.5–9). By sustained renunciation (9, cf. Gal. 5.24), self-watchfulness, and praying to Christ in the Spirit (cf. Matt. 26.41; Rom. 8.13; Heb. 2.18; 4.15 f.) we are to break the behaviour patterns that were formerly habitual to us (5–7). Third, as those whom God has loved, chosen, forgiven, and renewed to bear the family likeness (10, 12 f.), we must actively 'put on' the Christlike behaviour patterns described in vs. 12–15.

Questions and themes for study and discussion on Studies 26–29

1. 'Yet not I, but Christ lives in me.' Does this mean the obliterating of Paul's personality? If not, why not, and what does it mean?
2. In what ways is it true that God's service is perfect freedom?
3. What are the symptoms of religious self-indulgence, and how can it be cured?
4. Think out in relation to our various earthly passions (cf. Col. 3.5–9; Rom. 6.12) what it means to 'put them to death' (=*mortify* them).

CHARACTER STUDIES

30 : Rich Young Man

Mark 10.17–31; Luke 18.18–30

A dramatic incident took place as the journey to Jerusalem began. Someone came running, forgetful of all dignity, and kneeled impulsively in the dust. He was young, Matthew tells us; he held high office in the Jewish religious community, says Luke. All three evangelists who tell the story leave us in no doubt that he was a rich man, and by the common standards of society a blameless character. As Harold St. John puts it: 'he seemed to have all the keys of life hanging at his girdle—wealth, youth, prestige and a blameless character, but withal an empty heart.'

The Lord answered the young man's question with another. 'Why,' He asked, '*why* do you call me good?' The emphasis is on the first word. He sought to bring leaping to the young man's lips a glad confession of His deity. So He led Peter to blessing (Matt. 16.13–19). But here no answer came. The young man failed to rise to the faith that would have solved his problem. Imagine a pause after this verse. The Lord next seeks to elicit a confession of sin. He refers him to the inexorable standard of the law, which is 'our schoolmaster to lead us to Christ'. The young man is quite unabashed. He has performed the impossible. As touching the law he is blameless. He has been perfect since boyhood. It thus became necessary, as it was with the woman at the well, to touch the weakness in the life. The young man was shown that in spite of his eagerness comfort was his supreme desire. He loved this life rather than the next. In the pain of self-revelation he left the cross upon the ground, and went away with heavy steps. Looking after him, and turning to His disciples, the Lord said: 'How difficult it is for those who have riches to enter into the Kingdom of God!' The word in the Greek text is *chremata* which also means 'things'. The root is that of the verb 'use', and fundamentally *chremata* are 'useful things'. Wealth, in other words, is what we can use, and it follows that wealth is what we should use. It was the fault of the unprofitable servant in the Parable of the Talents that he hid away the money he had, and denied it useful employment. So it must have been with the young man in the story. His 'useful things' were denied their usefulness because they had taken the character of a soul that was dull and barren, and fired by no generosity or love. And yet Christ loved him, perhaps for the spark of that day's desire, perhaps with a wider pity than we, His followers, can feel.

31 : The Nobleman

Luke 19.11–27

The road ran down the east of Jordan to the fords near Jericho where the baptism had taken place. Probably from the slopes across the river, as the road descended, they could see the white mass of the Herodian palace among the green palm trees on the lush valley floor. The sight suggested a sermon, and Archelaus (Matt. 2.22 f.) enters the story again.

The will of the first Herod divided the kingdom which he had ruled so long, so dexterously and so ruthlessly. Archelaus, son of Malthace, a Samaritan woman, took over Judea and Idumea, by far the choicest share. Herod Antipas, son of the same mother, received Galilee and Perea; and Philip, son of a Jewess named Cleopatra, took Ituraea, Trachonitis and the associated territories in the north-east. Archelaus, who inherited his father's vices without his ability, adopted the title of king, and bloodily quelled disorders which broke out in Jerusalem. The result was a wider uprising, which required the strong intervention of Varus, the governor of Syria. It was at this time that the holy family returned from Egypt. 'But when Joseph heard that Archelaus was reigning as king over Judea in the place of his father Herod, he was afraid to go there . . . but withdrew into Galilee, and came to a town called Nazareth.'

It was imperative for Archelaus quickly to reach Rome, and to secure from Augustus confirmation of his position, before the situation in Palestine could be presented in too lurid a light by his many determined enemies. Archelaus' petition was opposed in person by Herod Antipas, who made much of Herod's testamentary incapacity, and also by a Jewish embassy. Somewhat surprisingly, Augustus declared in favour of Archelaus, though he cautiously denied him the royal title. The incident provided the background for the Parable of the Pounds, related by Luke. Archelaus was the 'nobleman' who went 'to receive a kingdom', and the facts were no doubt brought to mind by the sight of the palace which Archelaus had built at Jericho, where the story was told. It is a striking illustration of the fact that the incidental machinery of a parable is exempt from theological and moral significance. It remains a canon of such exegesis that the main point only must be disengaged, and no meaning attached to the pictorial and background detail. Archelaus maintained his stupid and tyrannical reign for ten years. In A.D. 6, a Jewish embassy finally secured his deposition and banishment to Gaul. (Herod I had built the palace at Jericho which suggested the parable. It was burnt down at the time of his death, but rebuilt and restored by Archelaus. The site was discovered and excavated in 1951.)

32 : Bartimaeus

Matthew 20.29–34; Mark 10.46–52; Luke 18.35–43

Mark, telling his story after the account of James and John on the Jericho to Jerusalem road, speaks of the healing of blind Bartimaeus. Matthew speaks of two blind men. If the three accounts are collated it would appear that the incidents took place as the party entered Jericho, and as they left it. Much has been made of these alleged discrepancies by those eager to find damaging 'contradictions' in Scripture. It is not careless reporting. It is the brevity of the narrative which occasions such misunderstanding.

If the three accounts are read precisely as they are set down, it will become apparent that three or four men found healing, one of whom was named Bartimaeus and whose name stuck in Peter's mind to be passed on to Mark. News spread through the town, and others sought the touch of Christ. Incidents therefore took place on both sides of the town. There is no need to suppose that the narratives have two Jerichos in mind—the old Canaanite fortress whose ruins stand outside the modern town with its jacarandas and orange trees, and Herod's city, which occupied the present site.

Bartimaeus, the 'son of Timaeus' as Mark obligingly translates for his Gentile readers, was a determined man. All good, as we have again and again had occasion to see as we have looked at the characters of Scripture, demands a certain eagerness, passion and desire. It is those who 'keep on asking . . .

48

knocking . . . seeking' who attain their desire. Elisha was angry
at the young king's half-hearted response to the symbolism of the
arrows. Lot's wife looked back and shared Sodom's fate. 'If with
all your hearts ye truly seek me, ye shall ever surely find me' . . .
Quotation and illustration could be multiplied, from Genesis to
the enduring saints of Revelation.

Bartimaeus set a fine example. He cared nothing for the crowd
in his desire to find Christ and the blessing He could give. He was
'importunate' like the widow, like the neighbour, in the two familiar
parables, indeed, after Zacchaeus' example. Observe the human
touches in the story caught by Peter's observant eye—the word
passed on to the shouting beggar: 'Cheer up! He's calling you',
the garment left behind . . . Dignity hardly mattered with such
salvation waiting.

33 : Zacchaeus

Luke 19.1–10

And speaking of dignity, consider Zacchaeus. The incident took
place in Jericho itself, and was rescued by Luke. Zacchaeus was a
fiscal officer. Much trade passed that way, for the place lay on an
east–west artery of Judean trade. At such points there were dues
to collect, and Jericho had always been regarded as a source of
income by Herod's house. There were rich balsam groves owned
by the royal house, and Jericho was looked upon as the winter
capital of the kingdom.

Zacchaeus could have been a man of considerable wealth, and
Christ may have been entertained in one of the finest houses in
the city. The buildings, colonnaded, and constructed round cool
courtyards, could have been like those of Pompeii. Zacchaeus was
the chief tax-collector (2) in this important place. For a man of
such position to climb a roadside sycamore tree to win a mere
sight of Jesus, was a remarkable action and indicates the sharp
concern for better living which drove him. He must have hated
the life he lived with its temptations, corruptions, and unpopularity.

Zacchaeus, like Bartimaeus, forgot all obstacles, and cared
nothing for the crowd. Nine of the ten verses in Luke's account
begin with 'and'. The copula occurs twenty times. Does this style
suggest that someone, gripped by the mingled humour, pathos,
humanity and triumph of the occasion, wrote the story in

Aramaic, and thus passed it on to Luke? If so we are grateful to an unknown chronicler.

Zacchaeus sought a glimpse of another, cleaner world, a world of peace with God and a heart at rest. He did not at first realize that such a world lies close to any one of us, and requires but a firm step of faith. The immediate delight of the rich outcast, incongruously up his tree, is evident. Christ cannot come truly as a guest into any house or life without cleansing it. It all illustrates two remarks in the earlier chapter (18.24, 27). And so the Lord passed through Jericho, the town which reeked of Herod and his house. He left it a sweeter place. Ahead lay the long winding road from the deep trench of the Jordan plain to Jerusalem and all that awaited there. The Lord was to know little peace from this day to the Cross. Zacchaeus gave Him His last quiet hour.

34 : James and John

Mark 10.32–40

Phillips has translated 10.32: 'They were on their way going up to Jerusalem, and Jesus walked on ahead. They were puzzled and bewildered at this, but went on following Him with fear in their hearts.' 'They were awestruck,' says Weymouth's rendering. 'They were filled with awe,' says the New English Bible. What is awe? It is, says the Oxford English Dictionary, 'a solemn and reverential wonder, tinged with latent fear, inspired by what is sublime and majestic.' There was a deep change in their Master, which the disciples could not miss. Luke, describing the same scene, remarks that, 'He set His face steadfastly to go to Jerusalem.' 'He made His face firm,' says the Greek text, as though to meet something formidable and unwelcome. Underline the thought 'they went on following'—in spite of fear.

The Lord knew what lay at the end of that long climb up to the city. He was desperately lonely. He had done His best to prepare His men for what was to be by the instruction of those weeks under Hermon, round Caesarea Philippi. But for all His instruction, how little they had understood! Fired perhaps by their own interpretation of the Parable of the Talents, they were excited at the prospect of an earthly kingdom, and the vision corrupted them. Truth, misconceived, can be bent into a lie.

They were no team, no band of brothers that day, but a divided group of self-seeking men. Nothing more awesomely demonstrates the patience of Christ than His response to James and John. He had taken them apart at some hour of rest by the roadside, and quietly told them again what awaited at Jerusalem—betrayal, pain, death, and resurrection. As though the words of direct solemn import had made no impression at all, the two brothers came with a selfish and ambitious request. 'Could they sit on either side of Him in the day of His power?' Without anger, without scorn, He answered them with careful sadness, gently disposing of their untimely selfishness. But consider this also. Anyone among the disputatious band on the road up from the Jordan could have abandoned lesser company and walked out ahead with Christ. Stepping on before, He found loneliness. In the same determination the Christian finds his Lord, and shares in the fulfilment of a plan. Preoccupation with lesser purposes holds us back from that full fellowship, half-heartedness, and lack of understanding . . .

Questions and themes for study and discussion on Studies 30–34

1. Was the rich young man sincere?
2. Distinguish the five Herods of the New Testament. The article 'Herod' in the New Bible Dictionary will help you.
3. Half-heartedness in religion. Read the letter to Laodicea (Rev. 3.14–22).
4. A new life requires but one step out of the old life.
5. Why were the disciples so slow to understand their Lord's teaching?

LIFE IN CHRIST

Growth in Grace

35 : Abide in Christ
John 15.1–17

Jesus' parable of Himself as the vine and His disciples as His branches shows how He in person is the Christian's life, just as Paul's figure of Christ as head and Christians as limbs (members) of His body illustrates how He animates disciples for His service (cf. Rom. 12.4–8; Eph. 4.7–16). Union and communion between Him and us are in both cases the basic thought. The Old Testament sees Israel as God's vine (Psa. 80.8–16, cf. Isa. 5.1–7); in calling Himself the 'true' vine (i.e. the real one, as opposed to that which was typical and imperfect) Jesus implies that He and His 'branches' are God's true Israel.

The parable, stated in vs. 1–8 and commented on in vs. 9–17, teaches that:

1. God the Father has His hand on Christ's disciples. He wants them to 'fruit', i.e. to be Christlike in character, hardworking in God's service, and influential for good and godliness (1 f., 8, 16, cf. Psa. 1.3; Matt. 13.8, 23; Rom. 7.4; Gal. 5.22 f.; 2 Pet. 1.8). Therefore He 'prunes' fruitful branches to make them fruit better (2)—that is, He 'cuts them back' through humbling and chastening providences, so improving their quality. Barren branches (professed Christians whose faith, being merely mental and not touching the heart, is in James's sense 'dead': see Jas. 2.14–17, 26) He cuts off entirely, by adverse providences here or judgement hereafter (2, 6). Thus He tends His vine.

2. The condition of fruitfulness is to abide in Christ (4 f.), as objects of His abiding love (10). 'Abide' means simply 'stay' (4, 6, 7, 9, 10), and the way to *stay* is to *obey* (10). Christ's obedience to His Father (10), in loving those He calls friends up to the point of dying for them (12–15, 17) is the model here: Christ directs us to love in the same way. Humility and self-distrust (5b), sustained attention to Christ's command as we move among men (7), and total reliance on Him for enabling grace, are all involved; we shall not be able to stay steady in Christ without them.

3. Those who stay in Christ may pray confidently and success-fully, for (*a*) their will and His will coincide (7) and (*b*) they may ask 'in his name' (16)—that is, invoking His authority as the Author of their right to pray, the Authorizer of their particular requests, and indeed the Father's Agent in granting them (cf. 14.14). To enter into this promise of prevailing in prayer, we must seek above all to know Christ's will; the major task in petitionary prayer is getting from the Lord Himself the requests to be made.

36 : Knowing and Growing
Ephesians 1.15–23; 3.14–21

In the first passage Paul starts a prayer from which the doctrinal excursion of ch. 2 diverts him. Chapter 3.14–19, following another diversion in vs. 2–13, completes the prayer. Paul asks the Father of the one Saviour and the one family (1.17, cf. v. 3, 3.14 f., cf. 2.17; 4.6) that his readers may *know* the wealth of their salvation (1.18 f.) and the greatness of Christ's love (3.19), and that, through this knowledge they may *grow*, i.e. 'be filled with'—so RSV, but 'be filled up to' would be more accurate—'all the full-ness of God' (3.19). The thought is of sharing, and so embodying, and thereby reflecting all the richness of life and all the moral excellences which God's work as Creator and Redeemer in Christ has displayed. As the 'knowing' is a corporate destiny only happening in fellowship 'with all the saints' (1.18), so is the 'growing'. It takes all the saints together to come to 'a mature man'—the RSV's 'mature manhood' blunts the point—'the measure of the stature of the fullness of Christ' (4.13–15). It requires the whole church to be Christ's fullness (1.23); He has more to give, and there is more in Him to be embodied, than any one of us can contain.

The realities which Paul wants Christians to know—that is, to know better than they do at present—make a striking list. First is the *hope* belonging to those whom God has called—the pros-pect, that is, of being filled up to God's fullness through enjoy-ment of grace here and glory hereafter (1.18). Second is the rich *inheritance* God gives 'in the saints' (i.e., in their experience, cf. the use of 'in' in Gal. 1.16)—a related thought, focusing on the notion of immeasurable personal wealth (18). Third is the great-ness of God's *power* towards believers here and now—power that may be estimated in part from the raising and exalting of Jesus (19–23), and the spiritual resurrection and re-creation which believers have already undergone (2.1–10). In the closing doxology (3.20 f.) Paul adoringly acknowledges that, just as Christ's love is more than we can know fully (3.17–19), so is God's power—but in neither case do the limits of our thought set limits to the reality. Fourth is God's *love* in Jesus Christ, of which we have just spoken—the love revealed in Christ's suffering for worthless wrongdoers and God's consequent quickening of them (cf. 1.6–8; 2.4–7; Rom. 5.6–8; 1 John 4.8–10; 3.1). The supreme need of Christians is still to know these things. But such knowledge is not natural; it comes through enlightenment by the Spirit (1.17 f.; 3.16), knowledge of the indwelling Christ (3.17), and a prior commitment to the life of love (17), and must be sought from God Himself.

37 : Man of One Thing

Philippians 3

Paul wants to enforce his summons to joyful exultation in Christ (1, 3, cf. 4.4) and total distrust of the 'flesh'—meaning here pedigree, privilege (e.g. circumcision) and performance (4–6). So he cites himself as an example (17) of one who had more reason for confidence in the flesh than anyone he ever knew, yet renounced it, and now saw all he once valued and relied on as mere 'dung' (8). The metaphor is coarse and violent, as it would be in a letter or sermon today, but it exactly expresses Paul's thought—worthless and unattractive refuse; 'droppings' to be left behind and forgotten (4–8, 13). All that was 'gain' to Paul, giving him as he thought a head start with God, he now regarded as 'loss', setting him off on the wrong foot and diverting him from Christ; so he had let it all go (8).

How came this mental revolution? Through knowing 'Jesus Christ my Lord' as the bringer of righteousness from God—that is, a right relationship with God (9, cf. Rom. 1.16 f.). This relationship, unattainable by the moral athletics of Pharisaism, is Christ's gift to those who trust Him. Paul was 'blameless' touching the law only by the Pharisees' external standards (6); Christ showed the inadequacy of these standards (Matt. 5.20–48; Mark 2.23–3.6), and condemned the self-righteousness based on

54

them (Luke **18**.9–14, cf. Rom. **10**.3). Elsewhere, Paul says that before conversion he was, inwardly at least, an active and lost sinner (Rom. **7**.7–11).

Knowing Christ brought Paul a new integration and purpose. He became a man of one thing (13), going 'flat out' like a runner in a race to know more of Christ and enter into the dying-to-live experience which is the Christian's road to glory, as it was Christ's own (10 f., cf. 2 Cor. **4**.6–12; Heb. **12**.1–3). With Christ as his path, prize and Saviour at the end of the day, Paul's life was dominated by the resolve to run for home which certainty of final salvation always imparts (20 f., 12–14, cf. **1**.6, 21). (What 'if possible' in v. 11 expresses is not doubt of the outcome, but self-deprecating wonder at it.) So to live, making each particular activity a conscious doing of the one thing at motivational level, and eschewing earthly-mindedness like the plague (18 f.), is a mark of Christian maturity (15).

38 : Practical Holiness

1 Thessalonians 3.11–4.12

'Holiness' (3.13) and 'sanctification' (4.3—and vs. 4, 7 where 'holiness' represents the same Greek word) are from a single root. The former means a state of being set apart for God, the latter the event or process whereby this apartness comes about. Paul speaks of God 'sanctifying' men in two senses, first by taking them into fellowship at conversion (so 1 Cor. **6**.11; **1**.2) and second by keeping them from entanglement with sin thereafter (so 1 Thess. **5**.23). But God's way of keeping us is to empower us to keep ourselves (cf. Phil. **2**.12 f.; Jude 21), and so sanctification is presented to us, not only as God's work (cf. 1 Cor. **1**.30), but also as our ethical target. So here. From this standpoint, sanctification means breaking with the world's ways to do God's will, and holiness means the condition in which this break has been fully made.

What this passage says about holiness may be put thus:

1. Holiness is *not optional*. Sanctification is God's will for all Christians (4.3). It is a matter of obeying instructions which come with God's call to salvation (4.1 f., 7); it starts with the heart (motive and inward commitment, 3.13) and is then expressed in

55

conduct. Holiness pleases God (1), but unholiness in any form sooner or later calls down His retributive action (6).

2. Holiness entails *avoiding sexual immorality* (4.3–8). The right course is to marry 'in holiness and honour' (4), respecting one's partner as a person made in God's image and the marriage relation as God's own ordinance of a lifelong bond. What v. 5 disapproves is not sexual affection as such, but using one's partner to please oneself rather than oneself to please one's partner—which was and is the pagan way in both marriage and more casual relationships. Clandestine adultery and overt wife-swapping are equally condemned by v. 6; in either case, the person whose partner is taken by another is exploited and wronged (cf. David and Uriah, 2 Sam. **11–12**).

3. Holiness involves *loving action towards both Christians and non-Christians* (3.12; 4.9 f.). Holiness is more than abstaining from all evil (cf. 5.22); Christian love is the way separation to the Christian God must show itself.

4. Holiness requires *willingness to work*, so as to be independent. Sponging and scrounging have no place in the true life of faith (11 f., cf. 2 Thess. 3.6–12).

5. Holiness involves *minding one's own business*, and not being a nosey gossip (11). How down-to-earth Paul is!

39 : On to Maturity

Hebrews 5.11–6.3

God made us rational and deals with us rationally; so every stage of Christian advance, from conversion on, is a response to apprehended truth. Where knowledge fails, progress with God is impossible. Chapter 5.11–14 complains that, after years as believers, these Jewish Christians were neither passing on the truth they knew nor holding it fast themselves (let alone hungering for more, as they should have been); instead, they had regressed to a sort of spiritual infancy in which even elementary things had ceased to be clear and they needed to learn the gospel ABC all over again. Blurred vision regularly results from not facing spiritual challenges squarely, and in this case the challenge to patience under persecution was not being faced (6.12; 10.32–36; 12.12 f.). In their self-induced infantile state, they could scarcely take the 'solid food' (teaching on Christ's perfect high-priesthood, with its implications of finality and exclusiveness) which the writer had for them, and gives in chs. 7–10.

What they lacked was *maturity* (noun, 6.1; adjective 5.14)— that is, the 'perfection' of the fully-developed, clear-sighted, whole-hogging spiritual all-rounder. The sign of immaturity was that they could not see that the ministry of Christ cancels and excludes the typical religion of the Old Testament, so that by reverting to Judaism, as they thought of doing, they would gain nothing (for they would find no grace there) and would lose everything (for they would incur supreme judgement for supreme sin in rejecting Christ: vs. 4–8). This blindness showed lack of capacity to distinguish good from evil courses—a capacity which requires constant consecrated exercise for its development (14, cf. Eph. 5.15–17; Phil. 1.9 f.). Regressing to spiritual babyhood, they had embraced fantasy and lost touch with spiritual realities. To lead them on to the maturity they lacked and needed, the writer resolves to leave the gospel ABC (which, to his own way of thinking, had been the area of his concern in the earlier chapters) and go on to the more demanding doctrine which, though hard, would do the trick if only they grasped it (6.1–3).

On the ABC (6.1 f.), note: (*i*) 'dead' works are those which bring death because they are evil (cf. 9.14); (*ii*) 'faith toward God' is the theme of chs. 3, 4, 11, 12, cf. especially 11.1, 6; (*iii*) 'washings' is probably a broad reference to the principle that cleansing is a precondition of access to God, taught by Old Testament ceremonial washings (cf. 9.9–14, especially v. 10) and confirmed by the symbolism of Christian baptism (10.22); 'laying on of hands' is probably a sign of welcome into the Christian fellowship, with prayer for spiritual enrichment (cf. Acts 8.15–17).

40 : Confirm your Call

2 Peter 1.1–11

God's calling (3, 10) is the main theme here. Note:

1. Like Paul (cf. Rom. 8.28, 30; Gal. 1.15; Eph. 4.1), Peter views God's calling as not only the sending of an invitation to life through faith, but also a work of divine power (3) eliciting the faith required and so imparting knowledge of Jesus Christ as Saviour (2, 3, 8, cf. 2.20, 3.18). Strictly, it is Christ Himself who

calls, not 'to' (as AV [KJV] and RSV) but 'by'—by the impact of His 'glory' and 'excellence'. These nouns epitomise His divine-human perfection displayed in the gospel (cf. John 1.14; Mark 7.37).

2. Response to God's calling, and the knowledge of Christ given with it, is Peter's key thought for understanding the Christian life. One must not be unproductive in relation to this knowledge (8); the unproductive man has lost touch with reality—the reality, that is, of his having been cleansed from sin by divine forgiveness, sealed in baptism, precisely in order that he might stay clean and keep God's commandment (9, cf. 2.20–22). The calling is to escape disintegration through unbridled desire, which is the world's state and fate (4); so the Christian must practise self-control (6). Again, the calling is to partake of the divine nature (4); so the Christian must imitate God by virtue, God-centredness (the heart of godliness) and love (5–7). Further, the calling rests on promise (4); so the Christian must be steadfast (6), focusing on God's faithfulness and holding fast his hope.

3. One's calling, and the divine election underlying it, are to be made sure—confirmed, that is, to oneself (the middle voice of the Greek verb in v. 10 makes this clearer than English can make it). How are they confirmed? By cultivating the qualities listed in vs. 5–7 as the proper companions, indeed fruits, of faith. For these are evidence that one really has been called to share 'all things that pertain to life *and godliness*' (3). Here is the biblical link between conduct and assurance. The passage is a good basis for honest self-scrutiny.

4. 'Supplement' and 'richly provided' (5, 11) are the same Greek word, meaning 'supply unstintingly', 'provide at whatever cost to oneself'. Peter is teaching that if we lay ourselves out to fulfil our calling, making an effort (5) so that its fruits 'abound' (8), God will also lay Himself out to fulfil 'richly 'His promise of final glory—a thrilling thought!

41 : Look Forward, and Grow

2 Peter 3.11–18

Expectation of meeting Christ at His return (whether or not our own death has preceded) dominates the New Testament view of life. Conduct is assessed by asking how it will look on that day when all secrets are disclosed (cf. Luke 12.1–3; Rom. 2.1–16; 1 Cor. 3.10–15; 1 Thess. 5.23); moral stability is enforced by reminders that faithfulness will then be rewarded (Matt. 24. 45–51; 1 Cor. 15.58; Gal. 6.7). Peter is on this wavelength (11 f.). He has four things to say:

1. *Hold fast the certainty of Christ's coming.* Then as now, some, disillusioned by delay, were sceptical and contemptuous of this hope (3.3 f.). Peter met their criticisms, pointing out that God's time-scale is not ours (8), that God has merciful reasons for delay (9), and that Christ's coming will in any case be unexpected (10, cf. Matt. 24.43 f.). His positive point is that the coming is a certainty because God has promised it (2, 9, 13, cf. 1.4). Christians must live in the light of this knowledge (17).

Verses 10–12 have an uncannily modern ring: what Peter describes is exactly like a nuclear explosion.

2. *Live in readiness for Christ's coming.* Those who expect it (12, 14) should get ready for it (11), pursuing holiness, sitting loose to this world's entanglements, and avoiding all that is disruptive among men and blameworthy before God (14). In this, as in cultivating Christlikeness (1.5) and seeking assurance (1.10), zeal should be shown and effort exerted (14); apathy and half-heartedness will not do.

3. *Understand the delay in Christ's coming.* Peter juxtaposes two startling thoughts: first, that God delays the day out of compassionate patience, so that more may be saved (9, 15); second, that Christians hasten on the day (12, RSV; AV [KJV] rendering 'hasting unto' is wrong) by the quality of their lives. With 'holiness and godliness' (11) may be included prayer (Matt. 6.10; Rev. 8.3 f., 22.20, etc.); both contribute to making the day dawn.

4. *Grow spiritually while awaiting Christ's coming.* Knowledge about Christ, and first-hand experience of His grace, should increase daily. Christians must not stand still (18)!

Note, incidentally, how Peter brackets Paul's letters with 'the other Scriptures' (16)—a most significant attestation.

Questions and themes for study and discussion on Studies 35–41

1. What are the tests of spiritual growth?
2. What is the relation between hope and holiness?
3. 'That I may know him and the power of his resurrection,

59

and may share his sufferings . . .' What would fulfil Paul's desire?

4. List the marks of spiritual maturity and immaturity.
5. What advice would you give to (*a*) a schoolboy, (*b*) a housewife, (*c*) a salesman, to help them abide in Christ?

CHARACTER STUDIES

42 : Reluctant Disciples

Luke 9.57–62; 14.25–35; Matthew 10.35–42

We have been following Mark and Luke conjointly as the story has been traced from Caesarea Philippi to the ascending climb of the Jerusalem road. At this point we must turn to Luke and collect a whole series of characters which are peculiar to his Gospel. Luke's ninth chapter might, in fact, have ended appropriately at v. 51 because at that point, and on through ten more chapters, he inserts a long tract of material not found in the other evangelists. The events seem to cover the last days in Galilee and on to those at which we have already looked in Mark's narrative, but we cannot disentangle an exact chronological sequence. We shall follow Luke to ch. 21.

In today's readings we meet some nameless men, one of them the scribe who, in a burst of emotion, promised to follow Christ. He had not counted the cost, and we are not told what he did when he was told the cost. Following Christ can often mean Winston Churchill's old price—'nothing but blood and tears and sweat'. He wants no one to follow Him under hope of material gain, under any illusion, false hope, selfish or ill-considered motive.

And He must come first. Hence the 'hard word' of Luke 14.26. The saying does not forbid filial affection. It is perfectly certain that He who bade His followers love their enemies would not have prescribed hatred for their parents. He was speaking in terms of comparative loyalty. He was speaking, too, in the colourful language of Eastern thought. Hyperbole is natural in Hebrew and Arabic. So also is vivid and concrete illustration. No eastern hearer of the precept concerning the 'second mile', and the 'cloke also', would misunderstand so far as to obey literally. They would readily understand that the figure of speech commanded only extreme long-suffering and sacrificial generosity. And all would see, with a readiness we exact and logical northerners do not find easy to understand, that the precept which speaks of hatred of one's parents means only that, when affections clash, loyalty to God must come pre-eminently first. 'Let me,' one has said, 'first bury my father'. He meant, of course, 'Let me

61

wait until my father dies'. Abraham had done precisely this at Haran. 'An earthly affection,' said the Lord, 'must not bind us thus.'

43 : The Samaritan

Luke 10.30–37; Colossians 3.11–15

The Jericho road ran through the ancient wilderness of Judea, and was a notorious haunt of bandits and terrorists. Jerome in the fifth century, and H. V. Morton in the twentieth, confirm that the evil reputation of the road was not confined to New Testament times. The priest feared ceremonial defilement if the still figure by the path should prove to be dead. The Levite was perhaps afraid of a trap. Modern men might similarly shun involvement in some down-town situation of assault or underworld strife. There is no indication that the victim was a good man. The Samaritan did all that which the others failed to do. As a visitor from the hated north, he lacked the Jew's knowledge of the Scriptures. Samaria had only the books of Moses, and it is ironical that Lev. 19.18, which counsels love for one's neighbour, was part of the Samaritan Bible, and was probably worn in a tiny leather case on the scribe's waist when he posed his question. The legalists, after the age-old fashion of their kind, had a way out of such obligations. They defined 'neighbour' to suit their prejudice and convenience. The splendid and challenging common sense of the Lord's reply cut through the clutter of their nonsense. We are free to deal similarly with that which darkens truth.

Thus it was that 'the Good Samaritan' became one of the best known characters of the New Testament. A good Samaritan, wherever he is found, and the commercial traveller of the Jericho Road has his vast posterity, is one who helps another even when the needy is the author of his own trouble. He helps regardless of race, caste or creed. He helps in spite of the cost. As Sydney Smith once remarked: 'You find people ready enough to do the Samaritan without the oil and twopence.' The Samaritan is a practical man in his beneficence. He acted first, regardless of consequences. We are not surprised to find that his credit was good. The innkeeper trusted him to make good his promise. He seems to have been a known character on the Jericho Road, and therefore was well-enough aware of the risk he ran, should the battered figure in the ditch prove to be a decoy. But are we treating fiction as fact? If so, what a tribute to the Lord's story-telling.

44 : The Importunate Friend
Luke 11.1–13

We have already looked at the Lord's prayer and observed that He was never more simple than when He was speaking on this theme. Some turn prayer into an exercise of meditation, into contemplation, or a species of self-therapy. Prayer, in the Lord's teaching, is speaking to God, an infinitely wise and loving Father. For some reason which eludes our human understanding He seeks fellowship with His children, and if these matters defy such explanation as human speech can give, is it at all strange that the Lord should resort to penetrating simplicities?

That is how this nameless character comes breaking into the story. It is a homely scene. The little village is silent and the small houses are dark, when the knocking comes on the barred door. The neighbour is neither thoughtful nor unselfish. He is con-cerned to feed his hungry, unexpected guest, and he knows that the man next door has a spare loaf. Hence the clamour in the street and the determination not to be put off. He was importu-nate indeed, a nuisance and a selfish nuisance.

Parables, as we have seen, are not meant for multiple interpre-tation. They have a point to make and must not be used to teach that which they were not intended to teach. The neighbour who awakened and besieged his sleeping friend was not like God. He was an awkward man to have next door. He may also have been a careless housekeeper. The Lord simply means that, in the common affairs of ordinary life, a man is not put off, if he wants something ardently enough, by the reluctance of another. How much the more, then, in the matter of prayer, should we pray with perseverance and invincible expectation. The importunate neighbour also had a certain confidence in his friend. Should we be less earnest with God, especially, as the last three verses stress, God is no sleeping neighbour but a father, infinitely more willing to give than His children are to receive?

And so an unknown man of Nazareth, of Cana, or some other

small place in Galilee, strayed into Scripture to teach a lesson, as he may have strayed once into the experience of Christ. Perhaps he was Mary's neighbour.

45 : The Pharisees
Luke 11.37–12.15

We have met them before, these religious leaders of the nation. They watched Him when His ministry began in Capernaum, caught up His words, and denied Him the synagogue. The washing which the Lord omitted was not a simple act of cleanliness. It was a ritual performance, regulated to the last detail, with the exact amount of water specified, the movements of arms and hands legally prescribed, along with the manner in which the water was to be poured, and the way palms and knuckles were to be rubbed and rinsed. It was part of the rabbinical clutter of nonsense which deserved the Lord's contempt.

Pharisaism, which had begun nobly in the days of exile as a movement to conserve and exalt the Word of God, had degenerated into such a pernicious legalism that life under its endless regulations was almost impossible without sanctioned subterfuge, and prescribed escape. Hence two damaging results. The practice of Pharisaism, as some conceived it, promoted hypocrisy, pride and self-righteousness. It also made little of the wider obligations and positive duties of mercy and love, as it wasted effort and fervour in the prosecution of endless regulation.

To reduce religion to a set of obligations and prohibitions, a pattern of attitudes, and a pursuit of rituals, while neglecting the committal of the whole person to God, is a common enough fault of man. By-products of such misdirected zeal are censoriousness for those who reject its enslavement, and a vicious self-righteousness. All Pharisees were not thus damaged. Nicodemus and Gamaliel were not men who fell under the Lord's stern indictment. Paul, in his days of Pharisaic zeal, sinned direly in his persecution of the Church, but it is difficult to think of him as a dedicated legalist.

There were good men among them, but their sin was, like that of the professional experts, the 'scribes', to darken that which was light, and to make a beneficent system a complicated and enslaving web. It is always and everywhere true that any system of religion, or any interpretation of Scripture, which makes religion difficult to follow, irrelevant to common life, hard to understand, and impossible for ordinary men and women, is wrong. Hence the Lord's denunciation. The 'common people', we are told 'heard him gladly', and this was because He brought God near, made Heaven real, and faith relevant to life. Those who, then and now, deny men this gladness, merit the words of His rebuke. Read also Matthew 23.

46 : The Farmer
Luke 12.16–40

The man whom Christ called a fool was a successful farmer. That in itself was no mean achievement. Palestine is not good farming country, save on the coastal plain and the great triangle of Esdraelon, where the confronting highlands precipitate the rain-laden winds of the Mediterranean. The brown soil of the valley bottoms is rewarding for the cultivator, but, for the most part, arid and boulder-strewn slopes offer grudging return for the labour expended. The Parable of the Sower gives a fair enough picture of the hard toil of the average farmer.

Nevertheless, the man in the story was a successful farmer. Good fortune or good management had made him rich. He had made his money by honest toil, defrauding no one, exploiting none. At least the story has nothing to say to the contrary. He also saw that wealth was meant to use. He knew when to take a holiday and to retire, and who was there rightly to grudge him his pleasures?

He was a fool, none the less. He thought he could control the future, not realizing how fragile life was. His farm should have taught him that trifles can destroy. He thought life was secure if he had a few barns full of corn. He confused his body with his soul. Life for him was 'eat, drink and be happy'. Happiness, he thought, was something that could be cornered and confined. Too insensitive to observe the crushing poverty of Palestine, un-conscious of the needs of others, he proposed to feed his flesh and so make life happy. He lacked a whole dimension of under-standing, and he must have cultivated this insensitivity by think-ing only in material terms. He imagined that he was in complete control of circumstances, and he mistook a means for an end. It would be difficult to find in one person a fuller list of follies. That night his heart stumbled, blocked and was flung into fatal faltering by one impacted clot . . .

He is a fool who fails to find a meaning in life wider than a shed full of food. What is life, this wondrous reality compounded of our hopes and fears, pleasures and pains, love and passion, tingling awareness, years like minutes, and hours like years, strife, peace . . .? It is, said Macbeth, glutted with his cruel ambition,

> . . . a walking shadow, a poor player,
> That struts and frets his hour upon the stage,
> And then is heard no more; it is a tale
> Told by an idiot, full of sound and fury,
> Signifying nothing.

'A narrow vale,' cried atheist Ingersoll, 'between the lofty peaks of two eternities—we cry aloud and the only answer is the echo of our wailing.'

Life is Christ, said Paul, a gift to share, a communion with the eternal. It is 'the childhood of our immortality, a quarry from which to chisel a character', said Goethe. It is a glory Christ came to give in unimaginable measure. He is a fool who misses it.

47 : The Faceless Crowd

Luke 12.49–13.9

We have thought, in an earlier study, of the crowd whose presence in the background of the story is so apparent in John's Gospel. We sense their reality in this passage. Christ's presence divided them, awakened them to life as individuals, and presented them with challenge. Christ brings peace (John 14.27), peace that passes understanding (Phil. 4.7), but He also sets men at variance. A new, demanding loyalty challenges some old allegiance, and divides those who were less worthily bound by it. Origen reports a saying of Christ: 'He who is near me is near the fire', and fire can never be approached lightly or carelessly.

The Lord besought them to look, think and choose. They knew the signs of the weather. The west wind rolled up the rain-clouds which Elijah's servant saw from Carmel (1 Kings 18.44 f.). Out of the Arabian desert and the wilderness of Sinai, the east and the south wind brought scorching heat. And yet, wise as they were in such matters of common observation, they shut their eyes to the 'signs of the times'. Like foolish people who rush to court, they were blundering on to disaster. And that disaster was in full view, as it is all through the Gospels and Acts. The Great Rebellion was looming.

An illustration follows, its relevance obscured by the unfortunate break between the two chapters which the reading straddles. Someone in the faceless, anonymous crowd listening to these words, calls out some comment on Pilate's Galilean massacre, and someone else mentions the catastrophe of the fallen Siloam tower. They were both tragedies which make some think of judgement, and others question the ways of God. Man, the Lord implies, is exposed to the vicissitudes of life, caught in some crowd on whom Pilate's indiscriminate brutality fell, harmed or maimed in the street by some sudden disaster. God does not always intervene to save the innocent. Goodness must be for goodness' own sake, not to secure some special privilege of protecting angels.

Nor has the Jew a special place. Hos. 9.10 and Joel 1.7 give the key to the imagery of vs. 6–9. The crowd would see Israel in the image of the fig tree. National enlightenment conveyed national responsibility, and failure to bear the fruit which God expected might lead to the withdrawal of privilege. It is a compacted narrative, but we seem to see the multitude, tormented, divided, ravaged by doubt, prejudice, racial hate—and denied a clear message by those who should have given it (11.52). What of the present day?

Questions and themes for study and discussion on Studies 42–47

1. The 'hard sayings' of Jesus.
2. The priest and the Levite on the Jericho road.
3. The importance of rightly interpreting the parables of Jesus.
4. The proper relation of the internal and the external in religion.
5. Do material things contribute anything to happiness? Be frank.
6. 'Sins of the times' in a modern setting.

LIFE IN CHRIST

The Word of God and Life in Christ

48 : Teach me Thy Way

Psalm 119.1–16

To our book-conscious age, the first thought which the phrase
'word of God' suggests is of printed scriptures. To the psalmists,
however, the phrase signified rather a body of divine instruction
('law', *torah*), written indeed for reference, but for the most part
handed down orally; a body of instruction whose very existence
was a sign of God's favour. Idols are impotent and dumb, but
Israel's God was both saviour and speaker, and Israel was
privileged to enjoy both His grace and His teaching (cf. Psa.
147.19 f.). God had declared His will in both senses (purpose and
command), and godliness meant precisely living by His word.
The grace and power of God's word is a recurring theme in the
psalms (cf. 19.7–11), with Psa. 119 (176 verses, all but one
mentioning it directly) as its richest statement. The psalmist
treasures the word in his heart and memory (11, 16), dwells on it
and delights in it (14–16), looks to it to keep him from sin and
teach him the way of life (9–12), and longs to practise it fully
(5–8). In this there is continuity between Old Testament piety and
its Christian counterpart; Christians too have God's word, the
two Testaments together, and for them too God's word is the
main means of guidance, grace, and growth.

Along with the *fact* of God's word, this passage indicates its
forms, viewing it from many angles. 'Word' (9, 11, 16) means
'message'; 'law' means instruction, as from a father to his family;
'testimonies' (2, 14), 'statutes' (5, 8, 12, 16), 'judgements' or
'ordinances' (7, 13), 'precepts' (4, 15), 'commandments' (6, 10),
are moral imperatives. Reference to the 'blessedness' of those who
walk in the law (1 f.), and the pin-pointing of 'seeking God' as
the heart of law-keeping (2, 10), are reminders that the word
includes promises (cf. v. 49, etc.) and reveals God Himself (cf. v.
18). The word is God's medium of communication and communion with man, in all the many-sidedness of His relationship with
us.

Finally, these verses show the *fruit* of God's word. It elicits desire for obedience (5), prayer for instruction (12), and whole-hearted seeking of God (2, 10); it cleanses the way, diverting us from what defiles (9); it moves us to speak for God (13) and find our joy in Him (14, 16). Thus through the word of God the work of God goes on in human lives.

49 : The Blessedness of the Righteous

Psalm 1

Psalm 1 is the keynote psalm, setting the tone and focusing the outlook of the whole psalter. It is a meditation showing the profile of the godly man ('the righteous', 5 f.), comparing him with the ungodly, and implicitly urging us to identify with him. The *blessedness* of the righteous—that is, their happiness under God's blessing—is the theme. Nothing said here is affected by the transition from Old to New Testament conditions; these spiritual realities are unchanging.

First, the *way* of the righteous (1 f.) is contrasted with that of his opposite number (6). The godly eschew the thoughts and plans, interests and attitudes of those who scoff at godliness and defy God (1). Instead, they delight in God's law. Why? Because they delight in God Himself, of whom the law testifies and from whom it derives. 'Law' here means God's instruction as a whole, including along with ethical directives covenant promises, and it is knowledge of the grace of these promises that brings the delight (2). D. L. Moody was right to say that either the Bible will keep you from sin or sin will keep you from the Bible; since God's law condemns sin, one cannot delight in both at the same time. Biblical thinking about morality, here as everywhere, resolves into a direct antithesis between God's law and sin.

The *fruit* of the righteous (3) is a matter of Godlikeness in conduct, influence for good, and positive contribution to others' welfare. In this sense, the ungodly are conspicuously unfruitful; sin being a disintegrative force, its servants bring themselves and the world only misery. The godly man's fruit is consistent and regular, like that of a tree rooted by a river and fed by the water in the ground. The picture is of God supplying through his meditation on the word strength for all good works (cf. 2 Tim. 3.16 f.). His universal prospering is inward; since he tries to do everything for God's praise, according to the word, he is enriched by the inner contentment of a good conscience, even when his endeavours are outwardly frustrated and abortive.

His *stability* (5 f.) is due not only to his inner integration, but to the fact that God knows his way, i.e. accepts and watches over him. In the final judgement he will 'stand', i.e. be confirmed in God's favour, while the ungodly, whose way is unacceptable, will fall (6). Scripture regularly evaluates ways of life by noting how they will fare at the judgement.

50 : If You Continue . . .

Matthew 7.24–27; John 8.30–37

Today, as when Jesus was on earth, His message remains the prime means of both grace and judgement, according to whether it is embraced or not. The burden of the 'words' (Matt. 7.24) which formed His 'word' (John 8.31) was the way of discipleship: how to live in the Kingdom of God under the King. After Pentecost, the apostles filled in much of the doctrine of grace by their elaboration of what the cross and resurrection had achieved, but they added little to the account of the life of grace, the 'Kingdom ethics', which Jesus had taught.

Central to this 'word' was Jesus' absolute and unqualified demand to be acknowledged as teacher, saviour and master (prophet, priest and king). This is faith, as Jesus taught it. In urging His hearers to 'do' and 'continue in' His word, He was calling them to the obedience of faith. Response to His call would be the mark of a 'wise' person, that is (as always in the Bible), a prudent realist who faces facts, thinks of the future, and picks out under God's guidance the rewarding, as distinct from the ruinous, way to live (Matt. 7.24 f.).

Continuance in Jesus' word is the only sure sign of being in grace. This is Jesus' point in the second passage. Certain Jews had 'believed on' Him in the superficial and inconclusive sense of being impressed by Him without yet knowing enough about Him to see what true commitment and discipleship were all about. Such 'belief'—half-way to faith, but equally half-way from it, and not always issuing in it—appears in John 2.23, and in the stony-ground hearers in the parable of the sower and the soils (see Matt. 13.5 f., 20 f.). Here, Jesus' very invitation to continue

70

gave offence: 'belief' evaporated and they wished Him dead (37)
So fickle can religious people be when faced with their real
spiritual need! Was it this side of Jesus' teaching that set Judas
against Him?

Unreality (because they were a Roman-occupied nation) and
conceit on account of their religious privileges shine out in the
Jews' words in v. 33. Jesus was offering them the freedom from
sin's dominion which Paul celebrates in Rom. 6. But they
resisted His word, turned the offer down, and thus established
their character as foolish men, heading for spiritual judgement
and disaster (35; Matt. 7.26 f.).

51 : Word of Grace and Power

Acts 2.41, 42; 20.29–32; Colossians 3.16, 17

'Grace enters by the understanding.' So said Thomas Aquinas
and the Puritans, and they were right. God deals with us, not as
sticks and stones or robots, to be moved by physical force, but
as thinking persons; and as such He leads us into maturity and
wisdom by stimulating our minds. More than that is involved,
no doubt, but not less. Hence God's Word, His biblically-
recorded message, read, preached, and understood, is the prime
means of grace. It instructs and challenges us, and is able to
change us, because the Spirit makes us attend to it. Through
taking in God's message, chewing it over and digesting it—the
process which Scripture calls *meditation*—faith grows and lives
are transformed.

This message is the word of the *apostles*, for they preached it
(Acts 2.41); it is the word of God's *grace*, for it declares His
redeeming love (20.32); and it is the word of *Christ*, who is both
its source and its theme (Col. 3.16).

In the first passage the Word is the basis of *fellowship*. Accepting the apostolic message opened the door to a common life in
which other 'means of grace' were shared, namely, the Lord's
Supper and the prayers. Without prior acceptance of apostolic
truth, however, such sharing would have been a hollow sham.
For there is only one Christ, the Christ of apostolic teaching,
and the only true basis for the Church's corporate life is a shared
faith in Him, based on shared beliefs about Him. This, be it said,
still applies.

71

In the second passage the Word is a means of *edifying*, i.e. upbuilding. Having warned the Ephesian pastors of doctrinal corruptions to come (30), Paul 'passed them over' (the word means this) to God, who by the word of His grace could build Christians up and bring them to glory despite everything. 'Sanctified' here belongs to the same realm of ideas as 'saints', and refers to God's act of setting men apart for Himself through repentance and regeneration, rather than to the consequent transforming of their characters.

In the third passage the Word is a source of *wisdom* as it 'indwells' us (the same word is used as for the Spirit's indwelling). The conjunction of thoughts indicates that the word will only indwell 'richly' in the context of mutual instruction and united worship, i.e. of spiritual fellowship. This recalls Wesley's dictum that there is nothing more un-Christian than solitary Christianity.

52 : Life through the Word

James 1.16–25

The New Testament descriptions of God's *logos*, His 'discourse' or 'message', make a fascinating study. The *logos* of God's grace in Acts 20.32, and the *logos* of Christ in Col. 3.16, here appear as the *logos* of truth (18; so called because it tells of reality and is 'no lie' (cf. 3.14; 5.19; Col. 1.5; 1 John 2.21, 27)). In v. 25 this *logos* is called God's 'perfect law', i.e. His full and final instruction in the way of life, in contrast with the incompleteness of the Old Testament *logos*. It is also called 'the law of liberty', the message that brings freedom where the Old Testament law had led to bondage. The thought that through God's sovereign action the message regenerates (18) is the same thought that Paul focuses when in Phil. 2.16 he calls the message 'the *logos* of life'.

God brought Christians to birth through the Word (18). James says this to illustrate the principle of v. 17, that all good things come from 'the Father of lights', the unchanging Creator of sun, moon and stars, whose ordering of the universe is the measure of His power to bless (cf. v. 25), and who through Christ shows Christians a Father's love (cf. v. 27; 3.9). As God's born-again children, Christians are the 'first-fruits' of creation in the sense of being that part which is given to God to be His sole possession and to be partaker of His holiness (cf. Exod. 23.19; Lev. 23.10–17;

72

Jer. **2**.3). These are the dimensions of the new dignity and destiny into which the Word introduces us.

God brings men to glory through the Word (21). 'Souls' are persons; 'save' looks on to the last day (cf. **4**.12). Here James states what v. 19 assumed, namely, that all depends on whether we are 'quick to hear' and receive the Word with meekness (i.e. humble acceptance, as from God), so that it becomes 'implanted' in the soil of our hearts. (Is there a capsuled reference in this image to Matt. **13**.1–9, 18–23?) Our receptiveness, in turn, depends on our total moral state—whether we are willing to clamp down on our pride and other forms of natural nastiness or not (19–21). If we are, the Word can save us both here and hereafter.

God blesses those who are doers of the Word (25). A religion of hearing and not doing is hypocrisy and self-deceit. To forget our needs which God's message exposes is frivolous, stupid and inexcusable (23 f.). To look into the Word closely ('peer in' is what the Greek suggests), and to persevere in doing what it says, is the only way to be blessed.

Questions and themes for study and discussion on Studies 48–52

1. Is it biblically correct to call the Bible the Word of God? How can this description be justified?

2. What is the relation between the Spirit and the Word of God in (*a*) the new birth and (*b*) Christian obedience?

3. What does it mean to meditate on God's Word? Find some biblical examples. How is meditation related to prayer?

4. What is the place of the mind in the Christian life?

5. How does our moral condition affect our capacity to receive God's Word?

6. Spell out what it means to be 'blessed' by God.

CHARACTER STUDIES

53 : The Woman and the Rabbi

Luke 13.10–17; 14.1–6

For the last time the Lord appears in the synagogue. Luke, physician though he was, spoke in the language of the day, and the 'spirit of infirmity' was a vivid enough way of expressing that feeling of painful resistance to all efforts to straighten her bent, arthritic spine. Touched with pity, the Lord healed her. It was the Sabbath.

The leader of the synagogue, a dedicated Pharisee, saw in the act a scandalous incursion into the sanctity of the day. He did not dare to speak directly to the Lord, another testimony to the power and dignity of His presence—so remote from the base and denigrating caricatures of today's imagination—but addressed Him by way of a rebuke to the congregation. It is well, in the affairs of life, to speak with frankness, face to face, and to avoid the craven innuendo. It was a piece of typical pharisaical 'play-acting'. Hence the Lord's strong word, for, as we have seen, 'hypocrite' means literally 'actor'.

Sham and posing always evoked the Lord's scorn. It is the very beginning of all virtue to have done with them and all falsehood. The scribal regulations for the Sabbath were typical of the legalism which had played a disastrous part in the corruption of the Pharisees' character. Provisions for the care and sustenance of livestock on the Sabbath laid it down that water could be drawn for ox or ass on the sacred seventh day, but that it must not be brought to the animal's mouth. To such meticulous absurdity could religion be reduced.

And as the Lord said, men such as the chairman of the board of ten managers who directed the affairs of this place of worship, could be anxious and concerned over trifles such as this, and have no mercy or pity for a woman with a bent, contorted spine. Human affliction and human deliverance were not their prime concern. They thought more of petty taboos.

Observe that the poor woman, in spite of her pain, attended the place of worship. This was a demonstration of the faith which found reward at the hands of Christ. The phrase 'whom

74

Satan has bound' is no concession to superstition, nor reproach to the woman. It is merely a recognition of first causes. All evil has an origin, and it is well to face the fact.

54 : More Pharisees

Luke 13.31–14.15

We have remarked that there were Pharisees of nobler character than those who murdered Christ. There were Nicodemus and Gamaliel. We may meet others of their number here. The Lord was still within the boundaries of Herod's territories, which embraced both Galilee and Peraea, and certain of the religious leaders seemed anxious for His safety (13.31). The lament over Jerusalem is placed in the narrative as a footnote to v. 33, and out of chronological sequence. The whole narrative, in fact, is sketchy, and the mere sequence, in Luke's mind, was not of prime importance. It is clear enough that these events took place as the Lord and His men moved down the east of Jordan, to Caesarea Philippi, and then on to Jericho and Jerusalem, and in earlier studies we have already followed them further along that road. Luke was working against time as he scoured Palestine for facts, while Paul lay in Roman custody at Caesarea. He was more concerned to record than to arrange, and for this his readers are grateful.

But meet now another Pharisee (14.1), the Lord's host. Why he issued his invitation (and it may have been in the region of Caesarea Philippi) we do not know, but the occasion was one of moment, and provoked a certain scrambling for places at the dinner. Looking on a trifle whimsically, the Lord expounded some rules, simple enough, but containing a rebuke for pride, the Pharisees' fundamental, and inhibiting sin (John 5.44).

'How is it,' asks C. S. Lewis, in his chapter on The Great Sin, 'that people who are quite obviously eaten up by pride can say that they believe in God and appear to themselves to be very religious? I am afraid it means that they are worshipping an imaginary God. They theoretically admit themselves to be nothing in the presence of this phantom God, but are really all the time imagining how He approves of them . . . this does not come through our animal nature at all. It comes direct from Hell. It is purely spiritual: consequently it is far more subtle and deadly ...' The whole chapter should be read (*Christian Behaviour*, pp. 42–47).

Another facet of the Pharisees' hospitality was its introverted form. They entertained in order to be entertained in turn. There is no reason why we should not thus share fellowship with friends, and the Lord implies no prohibition. He does, however, deplore the closed society, the building round and within religion of the social group, repelling strangers and intruders, an 'inner ring', after Lewis' imagery in another of his books. Let us be outgoing in attitude, mood and manner, and reserve some of our hospitality for such activity.

55 : The Reluctant Guests

Luke 14.16–24; Lamentations 1.12

The table talk went on. Perhaps the audience was responsive and in some way drew the Lord out. Observe those who rejected the invitation. The first man had urgent business, but his insincerity is apparent, for no one would buy land without previous inspection. He really wanted to enjoy his purchase, and there was nothing reprehensible about that. Christ's invitation denies us no legitimate joy. The man lied. His system of priorities was also wrong. Harmless interests, pursuits, pleasures become corrupted when they deprive us of Christ. The first man was a typical denizen of an affluent society, comfortable in his easy environment, satisfied with his earthly goods, and too shallow to think further.

The second man was not unlike the first. He was full of delight in his new team. He was anxious to see the brown earth of the valley bottom turning under the plough, as the beasts' muscles played in the harness, and pulled the share through the turf. A deep interest in one's profession or trade, concentration on study or work, all these enthusiasms and preoccupations are good. They are the marks, in fact, of good and worthy men. But these, too, can become too absorbing and deprive us of Christ. How common is the type among successful men!

The third man actually had the Law behind him. A Mosaic regulation freed a newly married man from military service for a year. With something like a conscious rectitude, this man answers that he 'cannot come'. Perhaps he is like the man who 'cannot' be a Christian, 'much though he would like to be', because the Church is 'reactionary', 'the tool of the establishment', 'out of date' . . . how the list could be lengthened! Or perhaps he had some substitute for faith in public service, in social activity, in political involvement. And too often the polite 'I cannot come' is, in truth, 'I will not come.'

There, then, they stand, so typical, so transparent, shirking the responsibility of committal, tenacious of respectable self-esteem and equally to blame . . . And there were those who saw the vital application to Israel. Israel had, after the Eastern fashion, received the preliminary invitation through John and Jesus Himself. The despised Gentiles, from the world's streets and lanes (21), were to take their place. Luke, travelling with Paul, had seen it happen.

*56 : The Prodigal

Luke 15.1–24

The story of the Prodigal Son is probably direct from life. A letter from such a boy to his mother comes from the Egyptian papyri. It was written at the turn of the first century and runs thus:

'Antonius Longus to Nilous, his mother, greeting. Continually I pray for your health. I had no hope that you would come up to town. On this account I did not enter the city either. I was ashamed to come for I am going about in rags. I beseech you, mother, forgive me. I know what I have brought upon myself. I have been punished, in any case. I know that I have sinned . . .'

Where was the 'far country'? Only across the lake opposite Galilee, in the Decapolis, where a million Greeks crowded 'the Ten Towns'. Gerasa, modern Jerash, is a ruin, one of the most imposing ruins of the ancient world, an oval forum completely ringed with pillars, and a high-lifted theatre, from which the audience on the stone seats could look over the heads of the actors down the pillared porticoes of a long and lovely boulevard, tall temples, houses, shops. They stand, a solid stone memorial to the city to which the boy from Galilee could have come on foot in a couple of days. 'He went into a far country and wasted his substance in riotous living.' Miles do not matter. It was a country far enough if its common way of life was set beside the quiet dignity of the old-fashioned household in Galilee.

Some itinerant Greek sophist, no doubt, had persuaded the lad that the Hebrew Scriptures sought to put the unknowable into words, that nothing indeed *could* be known that the senses could not tell us, that obviously life is physical experience, and that Gerasa offered scope and opportunity. What he did not tell him was that the capacity of the body is limited, if its responses and reactions alone are the source of pleasure, that today's philosophy is discredited tomorrow, and that by weaving words philosophy can argue itself out of argument, and destroy by words the validity of the words in which it communicates. The same Greek doubtless aided his cynical townsmen to fleece the country boy from around the lake.

Came famine. There are more famines than one in the stricken wastes of life. The rebel ended feeding the alien swine and found no pity in the pagan land he had sought in his mad quest for liberation. Fortunately, enough sanity remained to prompt him to action. He did what man must do, can always do, and will always be called to do if he will but stop, think, listen.

*57 : Father and Brother

Luke 15.25–32; Matthew 23.13

Back on the farm in Galilee the father waited. The view is wide from the Galilean uplands above the Jordan valley. The upper end of the fertile river plain is visible, tessellated brown and green and gold. The river, a blue sinuous line, winds south. The lake is a level floor to the east and north. The father often watched the road winding down the hill slope to the river. The highway passes through Bethshan, where the Philistines hung Saul's body on the wall, curves round the lake, and there enters the predominantly Gentile territory of the Decapolis. This, the waiting father knew, was the one way he could come home.

Parents, like the good man of this famous story, should seek to mirror their God. Then and now parents were not always so Christlike . . . And he saw him one day 'afar off', limping home in rags, 'and he ran and fell on his neck and kissed him'. The wait was over, but not the pain. There was an elder brother, meticulous in conduct, but merciless, jealous, and without an inkling of what went on in his father's mind, the very picture of the Pharisees whom Christ had in view. In Gerasa's oval forum they would have shuddered in their purple-bordered robes to jostle Greeks and caravaneers from the Persian Gulf. They knew all the rules of religion, every subtle detail of the Law, but knew no mercy, no care for the outcast, the underprivileged, the alien.

There are many such documents among the papyri, some of them almost savage in their expression of deep resentment against wayward children. The following, for example, is part of a deed of disownment in which a father cast off two sons and two daughters:

'Thinking to find you a comfort to my age, submissive and obedient, you in your prime have set yourselves against me like rancorous beings. Wherefore I reject and abhor you . . .'

The document runs on with legal abuse for some five hundred words. If the papyri are any indication, the father who killed the fatted calf for his lost boy's returning was gracious beyond custom of that ancient world.

Questions and themes for study and discussion on Studies 53–57

1. Why was the Lord so vigorous in condemning sham?
2. Hospitality true and false.
3. Modern excuses.
4. The 'far country' today.
5. The prodigal's brother. Can you blame him?

LIFE IN CHRIST

Prayer and Life in Christ

58 : Help!

Psalm 31

Strangely and sadly, many Christian people regard quiet contemplation of God as a higher form of prayer than making requests. Luther disposed of this idea long ago by observing that no activity so fully honours God as bringing Him our needs and asking for His help; for hereby we declare that, contrary to what we would like to think, we are not self-sufficient and cannot be self-reliant, but depend on Him at every point for all that is good. Scripture shows that all true prayer has woven into it some kind of cry for help. Often prayer is more than this, but never less, for our need and dependence are constant. True prayer is born of need.

Pain of body and mind, and the sense of isolation through hostility, are experiences which bring home helplessness and need with special force. Hence many of the model forms in God's prayer-book (for that is what the psalter is) are cries for help springing from these experiences (22; see Pss. 3, 6, 22, 25, 30, 35, 38, 41–43, 55–57, 59, 62, 64, 69–71, 77, 88, 102, 109, 120, 142, 143). Psalm 31 is typical of this group in illustrating two basic lessons—how much we need to pray, and how blessed we are to have a God who heeds our prayers.

Note the *covenant relationship* which David's prayer invokes. Ten times he speaks of God by His covenant name, Yahweh, 'the LORD'. He calls Him '*my* God', '*my* rock, fortress, refuge' (14, 3 f.), and himself '*thy* servant' (16), and these personal pronouns are covenant language, signifying the mutual commitment wherein the relationship consists. He asks God, his faithful redeemer (5), to save him (1 f., 16) in His *righteousness*—faithfulness to His promise (1)—in His *steadfast love*—mercy sustained in covenant (16)—and for His *name's sake*—because He is Yahweh, David's covenant God (3).

Note too the *confident reliance* which David's prayer expresses. Recognizing that he is wholly in God's hand (15), he 'trusts' and 'calls on' God (6, 14, 17) to save him from weakness within

(9 f.) and malice without (11, 13, 15, 20 f.), fully confident from past experiences (7 f., 21 f.) that God can and will do it, and freely urging other saints to 'wait for the LORD' (24) as he himself is doing. The covenant is the basis for the confidence.

The incarnate Son of God, the pattern of human perfection, was a praying man, and part of v. 5 was on His lips when He died (Luke 23.46). Surely the whole substance of the psalm was in His heart, just as it should be in ours.

59 : Father

Luke 11.1–13

The *necessity* of prayer, which the disciples assumed in asking Jesus to teach them to pray (1), is explained by Jesus' reply. Reason one for praying is our *needs:* through asking we receive (9 f., 13); those who do not ask do not have (cf. Jas. 4.2). Reason two, more basic, is our *relationship with God.* We are to think of Him, and pray to Him, as our heavenly Father (2, 11 ff.), because in Christ He has adopted us (John 1.12 f.). But fathers want their children to have a meaningful relationship with them, and this is supremely true of God, who both made and redeemed us so that we might know, love, and enjoy Him. So God's deepest reason for requiring us to deal with Him in prayer is that thereby we might get to know Him better. We should realise that as the Giver is more important than His gifts, so the gifts are given to draw us nearer to the Giver. Every experience of answered prayer should bind us closer to God.

The Lord's Prayer, here given in a shorter form than in Matt. 6.9–13 (RSV text in vs. 2–4 is right), is a complete answer to the disciples' request, for it provides the *perfect pattern* for all Christian praying. God must come first: we are to ask for the supply of our material and spiritual needs (3 f.) only as means to, and in the way that will further, the hallowing of His name and the coming of His Kingdom (2)—in short, His glory; and we must recognize that He will only answer prayers concerning our own needs in the way that actually makes for His glory. 'Daily bread' covers all material needs; forgiveness and protection ('temptation' means a *testing* which shows up weaknesses) cover all spiritual needs. Note that vs. 5–8 relate directly to the former petition, and 11–13 to the latter.

How should we pray? *Urgently*, because of our need, and *expectantly*, because of our heavenly Father's goodness. This is the point made by the parables (i.e. *comparisons*, which is what 'parable' literally means in Greek) in vs. 5–13.

Light on '*unanswered*' prayer is suggested by vs. 11 f. If a son asks for a serpent or scorpion (something bad for him), will not his father give him a fish or an egg (something good for him)? God reserves the right to give the best, and to answer the prayers we should have made when those which we have made are awry. 2 Cor. 12.7–10 shows how this may work out.

60 : All Together

Acts 4.23–31

No doubt the early Christians had held prayer meetings before (cf. 1.14; 2.42, 46), but this is the first one to be described for us.

'Free' prayer meetings are a basic form of Christian fellowship. Talking together to God, as these Christians did (24), should be as natural and spontaneous as talking together with one another. Prayer together for each other's needs should always be part of the pattern which the church fulfils of mutual support and help (cf. 29; 12.5; Eph. 6.18–20). Hearts united in praying, and then in praising when prayer is answered, are God's delight (2 Cor. 1.11). Jesus promised that special heed will be paid to prayers which express the agreed mind of (at least) two Christians (Matt. 18.19). To practise togetherness in prayer is a Christian duty, and should be a Christian joy.

This particular prayer meeting, and the line along which the Christians prayed, were a reaction to threats from officialdom (21). As always in biblical praying, they built on the reality of God's dominion, as Maker and Lord of all (24, 28), and with this on the Spirit-given revelation which He has embodied in Holy Scripture (25–27)—in this case, the revelation that the rulers of this world regularly oppose the king whom God has anointed (Psa. 2.1 f.). They prayed, not in hope of getting this situation changed, but in order to gain strength to live and serve God in it. Strikingly, therefore, they asked, not for an abating of the threats or leave of absence from Jerusalem, but for boldness to proclaim the word in face of opposition, and for further confirmation of their witness to Jesus' lordship of the kind given when the lame man was healed (29 f.; 3.1–10). They were thinking not of their own safety, but of the cause of God. '*Thy* will be done; *thy* kingdom come.'

It was the right prayer, and it was wonderfully answered. Pentecost almost came again! They felt the place 'shaken', in token of vast divine energy being let loose, and with the Spirit's power strong in them they witnessed boldly, just as they had asked that they might (31). Prayer for boldness in witness will always be answered positively, if we dare to make it. (But do we?)

61 : His Name, and His Will

John 16.23–27; 1 John 5.13–17

These two passages are profound and hard to grasp, for they lead deeper into the realities of prayer than most of us have ever gone.

Both show that the supreme experience of prayer into which our heavenly Father wants to draw us is not mystical ecstasy (some taste this, some do not), but is rather the joy—and joy it is (John 16.24)—of *receiving what we have asked for*. We find this joy, however, only as we learn to ask aright. The aim of prayer is not to force God's hand or make Him do our will against His own, but to deepen our knowledge of Him, and our fellowship with Him, through contemplating His glory, confessing our dependence and need, and consciously embracing His goals. Our asking, therefore, must be *according to God's will* (1 John 5.14), and *in Jesus' name* (John 16.23 f., cf. 14.13; 15.7, 16)—that is, it must express knowledge of both God's *goals* and His *grace*.

The context of such asking is *assured* faith. It belongs to 'that day' (John 16.23), when Jesus is risen and enthroned, and the Spirit has come, giving men 'understanding' to know God and eternal life (1 John 5.20, 13), and convincing them that the love they saw in Jesus is the Father's love for them too (John 16.27). In that day, when Jesus by the Spirit teaches them 'plainly' of the Father (25), no question of enlisting Jesus' support in prayer, as if He was more merciful than the Father or could influence the Father in a way they could not, will arise (26); for they will know that they, as believers, are the Father's beloved (27)— which is what Christian assurance is all about (cf. Rom. 8.38 f.).

83

To ask *in Jesus' name* is not to use a verbal spell, but to invoke a personal solidarity. We base our asking on Christ's saving relationship to us through the cross, and we make petitions which Christ, as we know Him, can endorse and put His name to—'that the Father may be glorified in the Son' (John 14.13). Then, when the Father answers, He gives 'in Jesus' name' (16.23, RSV)—that is, *through* Jesus as our mediator and *to* Jesus as the one who will be glorified, to His Father's glory, through what is given to us, Jesus' servants.

Central in the life of prayer is seeking to be taught by Christ through His word and Spirit what we should pray for. Sometimes we are permitted to know this more specifically than at other times and in other matters. 1 John 5.16 is an example of Christ-taught, Spirit-prompted prayer ('mortal sin', RSV, being apostasy). To the extent that we *know*, through the Spirit's inner witness, that we are making a request which the Lord has specifically given us to make, to that extent we *know* that we have the answer, even before we see it. If all this is a closed book to you, deal with God about it today.

62 : Praying for Christians

Colossians 1.3–14

Paul regularly prayed for Christians, and asked them to pray for him (see Rom. 1.9, 15.30; 2 Cor. 1.11; Eph. 1.16 ff., 3.14 ff., 6.18 ff.; Phil. 1.4–11; 1 Thess. 1.2, 5.25; 2 Thess. 3.1; 2 Tim. 1.3; Philem. 4 ff., 22). Praying for fellow Christians is a basic Christian responsibility. This passage helps us see how to discharge it.

Paul prays in terms of his knowledge of God's goal. The formula being applied in all his prayers is 'thy will be done'. From hearing of the Colossians' faith in Christ, love in the Spirit to Christians, and hope prompting both (4 f., 8), he knows they have been caught up in God's saving purpose (cf. 1 Thess. 1.3 ff., where Paul appears to infer election from faith, hope and love). So he prays that all God's purpose for Christians may be fulfilled in their lives, and asks God to give them four things:

1. *Christian knowledge*—knowledge of God's will (His plans, ways and commands) and of God Himself (9 f.). The Greek word used implies *full, thorough* knowledge, as does the verb 'filled'. In v. 9, 'understanding' relates to principles of truth,

'wisdom' to application of those principles in life. The construction of v. 10 shows that worthy living depends on this knowledge: he who does not know God's will cannot do it. Knowledge of God increases as one lives up to what one has already (10, cf. Mark 4.24 f.).

2. *Christian practice*—a life worthy of Christ the King (13), to whom we owe our salvation (14); a life pleasing God at every point and by every activity (10).

3. *Christian patience*—cheerful endurance of trying people and situations, with actual rejoicing as tribulation grinds on (11). Not for nothing does Paul specify that all God's strength and power and might are needed to produce such a reaction!

4. *Christian thankfulness*—gratitude for grace, the major motive of Christian living. According to 'the truth of the gospel' (5), Christian doctrine is grace and Christian ethics is gratitude, all the way.

63 : The Power of Prayer

James 5.13–18

Christians, says James, should pray for *themselves* when in trouble (13). Why? Because in prayer we look up from our distresses to gaze on God, the merciful Potentate who will in due course deliver His suffering servants (11). Thus prayer brings stability and strength; seeing temporal problems in eternal perspective cuts them down to size (cf. Psa. 73; Rom. 8.18; 2 Cor. 4.7–18).

Christians should equally pray for *other Christians* when they are in trouble (14–16). Invalids may ask that their pastors pray over them; elders must be ready to do this on request (14). This is not, of course, a magic formula for a cure: while Jesus' miracles show that there is indeed bodily healing for us in the atonement (cf. Matt. 8.17), Jesus' attitude to Paul's thorn in the flesh (2 Cor. 12.7–10) indicates that it is not His will for every Christian always to enjoy perfect health in this body—though when we get our new one it will be different! But we must be clear that the benefits of the atonement are one thing, God's time and manner for conveying them is another. Solemn prayer over the whole range of the invalid's needs is what James counsels, on the principle that illness is always God's summons to consider one's ways.

Such prayer may well issue in a healing which, like that of the paralytic in Mark 2.3–12, is a clear act of God, and proof of forgiveness (15). This will show the power, not of the oil used to designate the person whom God was asked to bless, but of the prayer itself. Such prayer for each other's spiritual wellbeing ('healing') should not be limited to Christian invalids (16).

'Faith' (15) means, not passive orthodoxy, as in James' *ad hominem* discussion of what 'a man' may say in 2.14–26 (see vs. 14, 18, 20), but active trust, just as in 1.6 and in Paul. James and Paul differ in cast of mind, but not in doctrine.

The efficacy of prayer depends on (*a*) uprightness of life and motive (16, cf. 4.3), and (*b*) whole-hearted and sustained earnestness (17, cf. 1.5–8) in the person praying, plus (*c*) congruity of the prayer with God's revealed purposes and ways (cf. Study 61). The story of Elijah (17 f.) illustrates (*a*) and (*b*) explicitly (cf. 1 Kings 17.1, 18.42) and (*c*) by implication (cf. Deut. 11.13–17).

Questions and themes for study and discussion on Studies 58–63

1. Why pray? List the reasons.
2. Do some prayers go unanswered? If so, why?
3. How should the Lord's Prayer be used in the Christian's personal life?
4. What can be said in favour of prayer meetings, and what do you think is the ideal form for them?
5. How should a Christian test whether he prays in the name of Jesus?
6. Under what circumstances can we speak of 'the prayer of faith'?
7. What is the work of the Holy Spirit in relation to Christian prayer?

CHARACTER STUDIES

64 : The Steward

Luke 16.1–13

This is another story from life told after the Lord's manner to illustrate a point. We could compile quite a list of such scamps from the Egyptian papyri. There is, for example, a whole letter file from the office of a petty official named Menches, from which it is apparent that he bribed his way to office in his village community, and used the small powers that his office conferred to extort, to manipulate and to embezzle. It is obvious that the trickster of the Lord's pungent little parable is no isolated type. The file from the Tebtunis crocodile burial-place, which exposes Menches of the early second century to modern scrutiny, is evidence that the parables were contemporary, relevant, and intimate.

But read this parable as parables should be read, disentangling the purpose from the pictorial detail. The parable in no way suggests that the steward's sharp dealing is to be admired. Look at the concluding verses more closely. The 'lord' (AV [KJV]) who commended the dishonest fellow was not the Lord Jesus. He has no capital L, just as the 'master' of the RSV has no capital M. He was the steward's own lord, his master, his employer. Rich enough to laugh at the loss of a few barrels of oil and wine, the owner dropped a word of grudging praise for the smart dealing of which he was the victim. And this was the parable's point. The rogue of the world will leave no scheme untried to win his end. The world will watch and grimly praise him as he turns the world's resources to his purpose. What of this spirit in a nobler sphere? Cannot Christians scheme as indefatigably for the Kingdom's sake? Should they not turn the world's resources into instruments of service? 'Make friends,' the Lord concluded, 'by means of the mammon of unrighteousness.' It is the legitimate use of money. And it earns its name. What crimes any coin may have taken part in! Its very silver may have been part of Judas' thirty pieces. It is poor stuff. But it can be used and turned to noble ends. If scamps can use it to build themselves comforts, cannot we use it for God?

65 : Lazarus

Luke 16.19–17.6

Lazarus, the beggar, has the distinction of being the only person
named in a parable of Christ. He may have been a well-known
figure, devout but shockingly poor. His sores were no doubt the
result of some deficiency disease, and his helplessness under the
foul attentions of the dogs of the street must show that he was
near his end when fellow mendicants took and placed him outside
the gate of an unnamed rich man. He craved to eat the pieces
of discarded bread that were used by the feasters on which to
wipe their greasy fingers. And none took pity on his desperate
condition.

The parable is highly symbolical, and follows the current
Jewish imagery of the other world. The story is not meant to
teach that bliss in an after-life is the reward of indigence in this,
or that acceptance can be won by charity. The rich man's callous
disregard of his neighbour's dire need revealed the hardness and
alienation of his heart from God and all good. Moses, and the
Old Testament at large, had stressed mercy and care for the outcast and the unfortunate. In pride and self-esteem the rich man
probably thought that his affluence was the mark of God's
special blessing. The rich man died as all men die. He was rejected
by God because God could do no other than say: 'Your will be
done.' The poor man was not saved by misery, for want is no
more a way to God than plenty. It is the grace of God, accepted
or scorned, which, then as now, produced the final result. In this
particular case the attitudes of two human hearts reversed earthly
circumstance. And note the sad prophecy—those who failed to
heed God's preached word, failed also to pay attention when One
indeed came back from the dead.

Observe that the prescribed reading covers portions of two
chapters. In the central portion of the Gospel there is little
attempt to set the events and discussions related in chronological
or geographical order. The note on Luke 17.1–10 in the Bible
Study Book series (The Daily Commentary) begins: 'These
crowded chapters in which Luke presents material from the last
discourses of Christ read sometimes like notes taken by hearers
or disciples. Indeed that is what they may have been. Much of
the teaching of the philosopher Aristotle survives in what appear
to be notes taken by his students, and only roughly edited. Luke,

eager to record and to preserve the precious words of the Lord, packed this portion of his book with all the sayings he could find, and the connecting thread is not always to be found. It is, however, there, more often than not. Forget the artificial intrusion of a chapter heading, and let the story run on. Woe, indeed, to such men as the merciless rich man who allowed a helpless beggar, one of God's "little ones", to lie in unrelieved and unpitied misery. Better by far had he been drowned before the years piled guilt's weight or burden on his soul.'

66 : The Grateful Samaritan

Luke 17.11–19; Romans 12.1, 2

There are three routes down from Galilee to Jerusalem. One can cross the Esdraelon plain in a roughly north-south direction, and proceed to the Holy City down the central spine of hill-country and Samaria, or else over the low pass of Megiddo, down the coastal plain, and up to Jerusalem by the steep road up from Lydda. Or alternatively one can proceed south-east across Esdraelon, pass through Bethshan south of the lake, cross the Jordan where it winds south circuitously through the wide valley floor, and seek Jerusalem up the Jericho road.

We know that this is the journey the Lord undertook, for He spent much time at Caesarea Philippi east of Jordan. Perhaps one reason why He took this route was the boorish attitude of some Samaritan villages (9.51–53), and perhaps, in a stricter chronological ordering of events, we might have expected to meet this incident earlier. We have already stressed the fact that Luke was hasting rather to record than to arrange.

At any rate, somewhere along the road which threaded the border of Samaria and Galilee, a band of lepers met Him, and found healing. Of their number, only one returned, and found in so doing a much wider blessing than the cleansing of his diseased body. And this man was one of the despised Samaritans. He alone was grateful.

Gratitude is a basic virtue. It reveals much of the soul's condition. It opens the personality to view. There are those who feel no gratitude for benefits received, spirits even base enough to feel some twisted form of humiliation if another confers a gift or blessing upon them. There are those perverted enough actually to sense resentment against some other person who puts them under an obligation. Such people touch the damning depths of evil self-esteem. To maintain such evil is to thrust the soul beyond all possibility of salvation.

The generous person in whom love, and all that flows from love, still lives, takes pleasure, not only in benefits received, but in rendering thanks for them both to man and God. It is better to err in the direction of too rich an expression of gratitude, than to fall under the charge of thanklessness. Gratitude, said dour old Samuel Johnson, is not to be found 'among gross people'. One in ten returned to give thanks. One in ten showed that he could humble himself thankfully to receive freely that which he himself could not obtain. One in ten could give glory to the Giver in simplicity and joy. How frequently in the talk of men, is unmerited evil discussed! How seldom is unmerited good talked about! One in ten found salvation, for one only in ten could thank his God. And he was a Samaritan.

67 : The Unjust Judge

Luke 18.1–8; Deuteronomy 24.10–18

Like the Unjust Steward of the earlier parable, the Unjust Judge is no image of God. Like the story of the neighbour who hammered on the closed door for bread, this poignant little tale aims at teaching determination in the quest for good.

There was plenty of corruption, graft and unfair dealing in the land. In his moving chapter on 'God's Poor', George Adam Smith showed how poverty was not only a state of want, but it denied a man standing, dignity, justice itself. It is wrongly said that 'prosperity is the blessing of the Old Testament'. There was, none the less, in Old Testament times, a damaging tendency on the part of many to look upon poverty, misfortune and loss, as the judgement of God, not to be countered by the mercy and the kindliness of men. We saw this thought haunt the attitudes of Job's friends.

How simple it was, in such a climate of opinion, for those with some breath of corruption in their lives to cloak natural hardness and uninhibited self-seeking with some perverted semblance of religion. Why help the indigent, if their helplessness was the will or the judgement of God? Hence widespread disregard for the rights of the poor and the outcasts of society.

90

The judge in this story had no theology to cover his injustice. He cared nothing for God. He was an atheist. He scorned public opinion. His like can be found in more than one ancient record. The oratory of the Greeks and Romans, their satiric literature, and the homely papyri of Egypt, alike speak of such characters. This evil man is drawn from life.

He met his match in a determined widow. She knew the law, and she knew her rights. She was vividly aware that, alone among the nations, Israel had care for the poor and fundamental justice written into the sacred Scriptures. She had faith enough to believe that such principles could prevail over human corruption, dilatoriness and procrastination. Day and night she besieged the corrupted administrator of justice to demand her simple rights, and obsessed him so that, in spite of his atheism and contempt for his fellows, he surrendered for the sake of peace.

God does not act thus in answer to prayer, but the Lord is moving on the level of popular thought. If grim determination and simple faith in the ultimate triumph of justice can produce results in a base environment, how much more can persistent prayer win its way and secure an answer when the Judge is the Judge of all the earth, certain to 'do right', as Abraham said, altogether good, eager to help . . . It is a true, vivid little story. We are left to hope that the widow won her case and lived happily ever afterwards, and that the unjust judge rode doggedly to his inevitable fall.

68 : The Pharisee and the Taxman

Luke 18.9–14; Isaiah 1.1–18

This is a finely told little story. Luke had it from someone with a vivid memory, and a gift for pungent language, which held and transmitted the spoken style of Christ. We can hear the Lord speaking in gentle satire and moving compassion.

The Pharisee is sharply drawn. He had his special place to stand and pray, conspicuous and self-advertising. He 'took his stand' says the verse literally. He was perfectly convinced of his goodness. He was 'separated' from the common run of men. He tithed! He scorned the sins of the flesh. He looked with searing contempt upon such men as the corrupted moneyman who had chanced to visit the sacred place at the selfsame time. He prayed aloud as the men of that age commonly did, just as they read

91

aloud (Acts 8.30). Everyone was permitted to know that this man was different, apart, good, accepted of God. And yet, says the Lord, he prayed 'with himself'. His words did not leave the Temple. God does not hear such prayers. They are noises in the air, inaudible beyond the failure of the sound-waves which carry their self-righteousness.

Not so the taxman. He heard the prayer of the hypocrite and accepted his definition. None of the versions seems to notice the definite article (not indefinite) which is in the text. 'God be merciful to me *the* sinner', he says, humbly accepting, without resentment, the self-righteous humbug's words: 'Yes, I am indeed the sinner he speaks about. He is quite correct in thus defining me.' It was salutary humility. He bowed himself under the condemnation of God, and pleaded for mercy. There seems to have been a deep and divine discontent among the petty officials of Palestine's occupation authorities. Perhaps Matthew, followed by Zacchaeus, had begun it all. The 'publican' in the Temple was another who sought some escape from a life of grim temptation, of vicious opportunity, of popular contempt and of agonizing compromise.

It was the duty of the leaders of religion to promote such a spirit of repentance, to welcome and to receive all who were disposed to abandon their chosen way of life, and to seek God and God's people. Contempt was no contribution to this salutary end. Pride is everywhere evil. In the holy place of God, and in a context of testimony, it approaches the blasphemous. But 'a broken and a contrite heart' God will not despise (Psa. 51.17) as He certainly despises all sham and all arrogance (Job 40.1–42.6; Isa. 2.12). Ritual practices and self-display weigh nothing with God. Giving, pious exercises, charity of this sort and that, are no substitute for sin unconditionally abandoned and the life committed in surrender.

Questions and themes for study and discussion on Studies 64–68

1. The Christian and financial responsibility.
2. 'The poor' in Scripture.
3. Ingratitude and what it signifies.
4. The disciplines of prayer.
5. Pride and humility in the practice of religion.

LIFE IN CHRIST

The Indwelling Spirit

69 : The Gift of the Spirit
John 14.15–18; 1 John 3.19–24

Before Christ came, God's Spirit was active in creation (Gen. 1.2), revelation (cf. 1 Pet. 1.10 f.), and regeneration (Psa. 51.10 f.). When Jesus said that following His departure (John 14.25 f.) His Father would give the disciples the Spirit, His meaning was that the Spirit would then start ministering to them in a new way. He would be *with* them (16), *by their side* (17, as Weymouth renders the words translated 'with you' in the RSV), and *in* them (17), as 'another Counsellor' (16, RSV), taking Jesus' place. 'Counsellor' is *parakletos*, a word with a wider meaning than any English rendering can catch; carrying the basic idea of 'one called alongside to help', it is used for an advocate at law and for anyone acting as friend, supporter and encourager ('comforter' in the old, strong AV sense). This is a personal ministry—which shows that the Spirit is not just a power, but a person, like Jesus, who sustained the Counsellor's role before the Spirit assumed it.

The phrase 'Spirit of truth' points to what is distinctive in the Spirit's new ministry: He shows Christians the truth about the glory of the ascended Lord, who is Truth in person (6), and so makes Him glorious in their eyes (16.14). Moreover, He mediates communion between them and Christ, who through the Spirit's coming 'comes' to His people on earth (18). Rutherford's testimony from prison, 'Christ came into my cell last night', is the best commentary on this. Here, rather than in any outward manifestations, is the heart of the Spirit's pentecostal ministry— the ministry in virtue of which He is called the Spirit of Christ (Rom. 8.9, where the small 's' in some editions of the RSV is wrong).

This ministry is permanent (16): the Spirit dwells with, and is in, Jesus' disciples for ever (17). ('Know' and 'dwell' in v. 17 are probably future in meaning: the present tense can be used this way in Greek.) There is, however, an ethical condition of enjoying the Spirit's ministry: those who will not keep Christ's commandments are disqualified (15, cf. 1 John 3.24).

The verses from 1 John appeal to the gift of the indwelling Spirit as proof that God (or, perhaps, the Son of God) indwells us. How do we know we have this gift? By experience of the Spirit's ministry of showing us Jesus' glory and drawing us into fellowship with Him. One who knows, loves and serves Jesus certainly has the Spirit.

70 : The Spirit's Law of Life

Romans 8.1–17

Having announced the theme of 'the new life of the Spirit' (Rom. 7.6), and then postponed it in order to discuss the way in which the law exposes sin without empowering for righteousness (7.7–25), Paul now develops a classic account of the Spirit's ministry to believers.

'Law' in the phrase 'the Spirit's law of life' (2) seems to mean 'principle', almost 'mode of action', as in 7.23. This 'law', working through the gospel, frees Christians now from sin's penalty and power, and will one day free them from sin's presence within them. Sin's *penalty* is done away through Christ's atoning sacrifice which fully met sin's claim, so that now there is 'no condemnation for those that are in Christ Jesus' (1–4a). Sin's *power* has ceased to dominate us (cf. 6.14), for we are in the Spirit, indwelt by the Spirit, walking in the Spirit, and 'minding' the things of the Spirit, i.e. the realities which the Spirit makes known (9, 4, 5). Those 'in the flesh' are strangers to this life, but believers are not in the flesh any more (4b–9). Sin's *presence* is recalled when Paul speaks of our bodies being 'dead' (doomed to death) through sin: we are reminded of his analysis of life in 'this body of death' (7.24), where sin, dethroned but not yet destroyed, still indwells and marauds (7.14 ff.). But one day the Spirit will quicken our bodies in resurrection, conforming them to Christ's (cf. Phil. 3.21), and then our vulnerability to sin will be gone for good (10 f.). (And won't it be good!)

On this basis, Paul requires his readers (12 f.) here and now to 'mortify the deeds of the body'—that is, do sinful habits to death—through letting the Spirit bring to bear on them 'the things of the Spirit', notably, knowledge of the purpose and

94

power of the Lord Jesus, and of the new life He has given (cf. Col. 3.1–6). This prompts him to speak of two further ministries of the Spirit to God's children. The first is *leading* them in the way of holiness and mortification of sin (14)—a ministry whereby He shows them to be sons of God. The second is *witnessing* to their adoption and heirship in their own consciousness (15 f.), so that instinctively they look to God as their Father and hope for His glory. Paul's 'I am persuaded' (38 f.) is a partial voicing of the 'triumphing assurance' that the Spirit's witness brings; in a fuller sense, the whole chapter is voicing it.

71 : Walk in the Spirit

Galatians 5.13–26

Galatians declares how Christians have exchanged the bondage of legal religion for the freedom of life in the Spirit (2.19 f.; 3.2 f.; 5.1, 5 f., 13; 6.15). Not by works but by faith—not by the law but by the Spirit—not by circumcision but by new creation— not in bondage but in freedom—these are the antitheses on which Paul's argument about the making of Christians turns. Here he adds a further antithesis about the conduct ('walk', 16, 25) of Christians: be led, he says, not by the flesh but by the Spirit. 'Flesh' (16, 17, 19, 24) means, not our bodies or humanity as such, but the 'indwelling sin' of Rom. 7.7–25, the energy of our fallenness in Adam. Paul's main points are these:

1. *The commitment of the Christian brings conflict.* Christians have denied what the Puritans called 'carnal self' in order to be 'led by the Spirit' (18); they have 'crucified the flesh' (24) in the sense of renouncing its ways, wishing it dead, and asking Jesus to kill it. This is the essence of repentance. But conflict arises at once, for the flesh, though doomed, is not dead yet. Desires prompted by the indwelling Spirit, and impulses springing from sin (including distaste for the Spirit's promptings) pull against each other (cf. Rom. 7.14–25 again), so that the Christian is never free from a degree of inner tension and frustration. The last words of v. 17 do not mean that he cannot do any good that he would, only that he can never do enough of it to satisfy him and always achieves less than he hoped for, inasmuch as somewhere within him the brakes went on and the steering-wheel of motive and purpose got twisted.

2. *The indwelling of the Spirit brings Christlikeness*. Refusing to gratify the flesh (16) is the negative side of sanctification; its positive side is the building up of Christian character and habits, with love to one's neighbour crowning everything (22 f., 13 f.). 'Fruit' is singular, for the nine graces mentioned unite to form one thing, the image of Jesus (cf. 2 Cor. 3.18). Paul's metaphor embodies the thought that the Christlikeness which the Spirit enables us to exhibit reveals the new creation in Christ of our innermost self, that transforming work of grace whereby the bad tree was made capable of producing good fruit (see Matt. 7.17 f.; 12.33).

72 : Gratify the Spirit

Ephesians 4.25–32; 5.15–20

In Ephesians God's gift of the indwelling Spirit is pictured as His 'seal' set upon Christians to mark them out as His (cf. 2 Cor. 1.22). The picture points forward to the day when God will claim His property, thus sealed, and take believers out of the realm of sin and death for ever (Eph. 1.13 f.; 4.30). The word 'redemption', meaning 'rescue' and implying a ransom, is used of this hope in 4.30, as in Rom. 8.23, though its commoner reference is to present forgiveness through the cross, as in Eph. 1.7.

In the first three chapters, Paul spoke of the Spirit's work in giving knowledge of God (1.17; 3.5, 16–19) and fellowship with Him (2.18, 22); in the last three, the burden of all references to the Spirit is ethical.

The plea against *grieving* the Spirit (4.30) is a witness both to the Spirit's personality and to the fact that divine holiness is His nature (which is why He is called the *Holy* Spirit). As with the first and second Persons of the Godhead, so with the third—some ways of behaving please Him, others distress and offend Him. In the second category come the lapses mentioned in v. 31, and stealing (28), and in short all transgressions of the moral law. For Christians to fall into these sins grieves the Spirit because it directly thwarts His purpose and spoils His work of making us Christlike. Knowledge that our bodies are temples of the Holy Spirit (1 Cor. 6.19), and that this 'gracious, willing Guest' is hard at work in our hearts to sanctify us, should induce the 'fear and trembling' of Phil. 2.12 ('reverent awe' is the meaning) and quickly shame us out of any moral laxity.

To this dissuasive against grieving the Spirit the call to be *filled* with the Spirit (5.18) is the positive counterpart. The imperative is in the present tense, implying a constant obligation. 'Filled' conveys the thought of being wholly concerned with, and wholly controlled by, the realities which the Spirit makes known, and the ideal of life to which He points us. The question which vs. 18–20 raise and answer is, from what source should satisfaction be sought? Not from indulgence in alcohol (the worldling's way of trying to raise his enjoyment level), but from being occupied entirely with the Spirit's concerns. Then we shall have something to sing about! (19)—for the gratified Holy Spirit will sustain in us a joy which the worldling never knows (cf. Rom. 14.17).

Questions and themes for study and discussion on Studies 69–72

1. What differences, if any, were there between the Holy Spirit's ministry to the apostles and His ministry to us?
2. How does the Spirit bear witness to us that we are children of God?
3. How from the Scriptures would you counsel a Christian who wanted to be filled with the Holy Spirit?
4. Under what conditions can one claim to be 'led by the Spirit'?
5. 'Honour the Holy Spirit' (Evan Roberts). What do these passages suggest to you in the way of steps to be taken by those who would do as Roberts said?

CHARACTER STUDIES

73 : The Owner of the Ass

Luke 19.29–48; Zechariah 9.9

We return to the story of the Jericho road which we followed in Mark's narrative. The long climb to Jerusalem reached its highest point where the road crossed the Mount of Olives. The modern highway skirts it, but in ancient times the approach seems to have been designed to give the incoming pilgrim a grand view of the city. It lies across the valley on its plateau, tilted like a shield, and from the summit of the Mount the magnificent pile of Herod's Temple must have been a feature of the foreground.

As the Lord looked, His mind seemed to pierce the veil of forty years and He saw the sight as Vespasian and Titus were to see it, the slopes seared and devastated, the gates closed, the walls manned, the earth littered with rubble and ballista stones, and the streets full of the dead killed by famine and internecine strife.

Jerusalem was to choose Barabbas, and this was to be the end, but it was not to come without His earnest offer of God's peace. He deliberately chose to fulfil the oracle of Zechariah, and enter the passionate, rebellious place riding on an ass, the symbol of peace. On such terms He was to offer Himself. He had said nothing to His men. Their lamentable strife down the Jericho road gave little hope that they would understand. Knowing the Old Testament, they should, like the rest of Jerusalem, have found the message plain.

Bethphage and Bethany lie just over the brow of the hill on the side of the Jordan road, and somewhere here lived a man who played a part in the story. The Lord must have had an arrangement with him to borrow an ass with which to stage His eloquent piece of Old Testament symbolism. This nameless character in the events of the King's coming is typical of many in the story of the New Testament and the Church, the men and women known only to God who are vital links in a chain. There is immense encouragement in the thought for the multitude of those who have little place in the records of men, but who have been God's workmen in tasks of eternal significance.

We saw in the story of the loaves and fishes the same divine

98

principle. God's acts seem so often to depend upon some shred of human help. He enters life and history through the bridgehead of some human surrender, the bread placed in His creative hands, the submission of some Mary, the loan of an ass . . . The nameless man of Bethphage or Bethany played his part and slipped back into the host of those who will one day find a name, a recognition and a reward.

74 : The Husbandmen
Luke 20.1–18; Isaiah 5.1–7

The Lord sought the Temple court for the next few days of teaching. He cleared the sacred place again of its clutter of evil, but the hucksters were not the only ones who defiled its sanctity. A group from the Sanhedrin 'came upon him'. Luke uses the same verb as that which he used in 10.40 of Martha's descent upon the Lord and Mary. They stood over Him, determined to discredit His authority. They were desperately fumbling for a charge against Him and found themselves frustrated to the point that their questions ceased (40).

Observe His method. He countered question with question. He carried the assault into the enemy's territory. If such a strife of words is thrust upon a Christian in debate, in television interview, or in unavoidable public controversy, it is well to apply the method. There is no need to stand backed against a wall. The offensive should alternate with defensive. Thrust must succeed parry. Be ready, by all means, to return the 'reasoned answer', as Peter enjoins (1 Pet. 3.15), but let question succeed question. The opponent of the gospel has many serious questions to answer, and should be compelled, if he chooses argument, to answer them. He also has a faith to defend, and for which he must give a reason, for he too has staked his life upon a belief—in chance as his God, in chaos for his view of life, in annihilation as the end.

The satiric picture of those who should have kept the vineyard for its master was devastating comment. The image is deep in the Old Testament. The Bible Study Book (The Daily Commentary) on Luke comments: 'History was woven bitingly into the story. Those who were entrusted with the guardianship of the vineyard looked upon it as their private preserve, and neither Israel nor

Israel's rulers, who were the twin objects of the parable's twofold
significance, held a prerogative here. The parable passed from
history to prophecy in vs. 14, 15. Verse 17 is from Psa. 118.22, a
song said to have been sung at the completion of the walls of
Jerusalem in 444 B.C. The Lord showed the true content of the
words. The Early Church remembered this—see Acts 4.11;
1 Pet. 2.7 f.; Rom. 9.33.'

So ended Tuesday of Holy Week (Mark 11.12, 20, 27).

75 : Tiberius Caesar

Luke 20.19–26

A coin lay in the Lord's hand, probably a silver denarius of
Tiberius, and that stern Roman visage, side-faced on the palm
of Christ, speaks of another character of Scripture. Augustus'
stepson, a competent soldier and administrator, Tiberius came
to power at the age of fifty-six because Augustus could find no
other. Naturally suspicious, embittered by such treatment, and
unlovable by nature, Tiberius suffered much at the hands of
circumstance. His trusted minister Seianus, head of the household troops, and probably the patron of Pilate, betrayed him,
and was struck down by the old emperor in his last years, in
one of his few popular acts.

Tiberius also found Tacitus as an historian, a writer of mordant
power, who blamed him for the evils of Domitian's reign under
whom he, like John and the Church, suffered. It has been difficult
for modern historians to find the record of the real achievements
of his rule. Tiberius handled power clumsily. Heredity and
environment conspired to make him dour and unsociable. It is
easy to blame and vilify such personalities, less simple to com-
mend and grant the justice of fair appraisal.

It is difficult to bear firmly in mind while reading Tacitus' vivid
narrative of Tiberius' time, that the Roman world at large was
still tranquil in the peace which Augustus had established. The
frontiers were adequately maintained, and the Parthians,
perennial problem of the north-east, had no cause to suspect
that weak hands held the weapons of Rome. History, as Rome
recorded it, was, of course, centred on the Tiber, for a picture
of life as men at large lived it, one must turn to the multitude of
inscriptions which archaeology diligently collects and records, to

papyri from Egypt, and to those small books which classical historians too commonly overlook as documents of the first two Roman principates, the four Gospels of the New Testament, and the opening chapters of the Acts of the Apostles. Christ was born under Augustus, and 'suffered under Pontius Pilatus', Tiberius' steward. The Church was founded and first organized under the same prince.

His 'graven image', stamped on the elegant bright coin, and the occasion of the Jews' hatred, heard one of the great sayings of all time: 'Give back to Caesar what Caesar owns, but give back to God that which is His . . .'

76 : The Sadducees

Luke 20.27–38; 1 Corinthians 15.12–19

The Sadducees were a worldly sect who had cornered the prestige, the possessions and the emoluments of the priesthood. They accepted only the five books of Moses, and so, among the vital doctrines they were constrained to reject, they abandoned all belief in a resurrection and an after-life (Acts 23.6–10). Belief determines conduct. With no thought of judgement to come, the Sadducee found it easy to turn the Temple court into a sordid place of merchandise. He found no impediment to murder, when an awkward Galilean disturbed, or was thought likely to disturb, the relationship of compromise and collaboration which had been worked out with the occupying forces. Life must be viewed in the light of eternity, if life is to be viewed whole. Distort, narrow or corrupt the full doctrine of the eternal hope and ultimate responsibility, and vicious twists are formed in matters of morals and daily living.

The Sadducees were ignorant as well as worldly. Learning was with the Pharisees and the scribes. The Sadducee rejected a whole culture along with his rejection of great tracts of the Old Testament. It is the way of ignorant men to be supercilious in argument, and to attack by ridicule. They sought to make the teaching of Christ appear absurd, and argued with crass insincerity. Accepting Moses, they professed also to accept the existence of God, and found themselves on the horns of a dilemma concerning both Moses and the living God.

The Sadducees remain a type of worldly-minded priests. The

101

world has had enough of them. To lose a faith is tragedy enough. To lose the keen edge of conviction, and find the message, which ardour once sought to communicate, crumble in the hands, is a bitter experience too often encountered by those who seek Christian usefulness through a gauntlet of decayed theology in those places where training is sought. Such loss falls short of sin, and sometimes finds remedy. But sin it is, and, if the Lord's words have authority, sin past forgiving, to continue to hold the status and emoluments of office when the reason for holding office is gone. And if the resurrection is folly, deceit or superstition, what gospel, as Paul said, what Church, what message or reason for preaching remains?

77 : The Widow

Luke 21.1–19

Sitting in the Temple, weary with battling the legalism, the treachery and the apostasy of those in whose hands lay the religion of Israel, the Lord 'looked up and saw' a sight which gladdened His tired eyes. A woman cast a tiny coin into the treasury chute. The '*lepton*' ran over one hundred to the denarius, but God does not measure gifts by the standards of men.

Here first of all was another member of the Remnant. Amid the vast betrayal of the 'shepherds of Israel', the common people of the land still retained their faithful. Here was one of them. A widow in that hard world had a grim life. It proved one of the first requirements of the Church, as both the story in Acts and the Pastoral Epistles show, to make merciful provision for widows. The tale of Ruth illustrated the same need. Sacrifice, therefore, there must have been in the giving of the one small coin.

But consider the implications. Without knowing it, an unknown woman had slipped into the story and out again, bringing encouragement to the wounded Christ. She also performed the function we have observed before—that of providing God with that small fragment which enables Him to invade some tract of human life. The *lepton* of the day's giving has been mightily productive. The sacrifice which it represented has stirred to action a multitude with far more to give but no greater generosity.

And, slipping back into the Jerusalem crowd the nameless

woman taught another lesson. True service is not necessarily spectacular. It is *not* measured by the applause, the estimation or the regard of men. It *is* measured by the applause, the estimation and the regard of God. It is measured by devotion. The tiny coin was a symbol. It was a sign of a surrendered soul. James Russell Lowell, the American poet, invented a story to add to the Arthur Saga. It was about Sir Launfal, the knight who found that the Holy Grail was a cup which he used for a beggar's need. He concludes:

> *In many climes, without avail,*
> *Thou hast spent thy life for the Holy Grail;*
> *Behold, it is here—this cup which thou*
> *Didst fill at the streamlet for Me but now;*
> *This crust is My body broken for thee,*
> *This water His blood that died on the tree;*
> *The Holy Supper is kept, indeed,*
> *In whatso we share with another's need;*
> *Not what we give, but what we share,*
> *For the gift without the giver is bare;*
> *Who gives himself with his alms feeds three,*
> *Himself, his hungering neighbour and me.*

Read sometime *The Vision of Sir Launfal.*

78 : The Foolish Virgins

Luke 21.20–38; Matthew 25.1–13

First of all grasp the point of the parable. It is absurd to imagine that the refusal of the wise to share their resources with the foolish in an emergency sanctions selfishness. We have seen that it is always good exegesis to limit the meaning of a parable to the specific purpose for which it was constructed. In the accepted manner of the east, the Lord taught by means of vivid pictures from real life. Some of the details are designed to colour the picture. Others contribute to the didactic end in view. That end must be carefully considered. The parable of the virgins is designed to teach the need for spiritual preparedness for every soul awaiting the coming of the Lord. It is designed, too, to show that in such matters we cannot live on another's experience. The oil signifies that unction of the soul that feeds the living flame of devotion, zeal and spiritual fitness. It is the gift of God's anointing, and the fruit of willing faith. No one else can get it for us. If our religion is merely dry-souled fellowship with a social group, it will fail us in the ultimate realities. The experience others have won cannot then, at a moment's notice, be transferred effectively to us, and if we were to press the meaning of the story one step further, it would be to suggest that it speaks of judgement. A crisis finds all asleep, indistinguishable as wheat and tares. But a crisis sifts and judges the souls of men. Those who had known reality respond.

Here are some characters of Scripture too common for our comfort. It is the commonest of human faults to put off consideration of vital matters until it is too late. The voiceless, silent, uncommitted, faceless majority are everywhere and in all times. All that is required for the triumph of evil is for the good to do nothing. They only meet the demands of a compelling moment who in times past have prepared their soul for the response. Delay is deadly. The whole trend of modern life is directed to the avoidance of all consideration of ultimate questions.

> *Tomorrow, and tomorrow, and tomorrow,*
> *Creeps in this petty pace from day to day,*
> *To the last syllable of recorded time;*
> *And all our yesterdays have lighted fools*
> *The way to dusty death.*

How right was the disillusioned Macbeth.

Questions and themes for study and discussion on Studies 73–78

1. The unnamed allies of Christ.
2. The attack on the Christian today.
3. What must we 'render to Caesar' today?
4. The resurrection—fact or fantasy?—literal truth or symbol?
5. 'The gift without the giver is bare.'
6. 'Avoiding ultimate questions.'

LIFE IN CHRIST

Christian Fellowship

79 : Love One Another

John 13.34–35; 1 John 3.10–18

Jesus told His disciples to love each other (John 13.34; 1 John 3.11). But love is an elastic and problematical word; what should 'loving' involve? Jesus answered this question, and set the sights of Christian love for all time, by adding: 'as I have loved you'. The measures of love are how much it gives, how free it is from selfish motives, how much it puts up with, and how long it lasts. Jesus' love gave to the uttermost (for Him, the cost of loving was Calvary). It was totally selfless (look at Gethsemane). It was infinitely patient (Jesus' sweetness with His silly disciples is breathtaking). And it was, and is, unending. This is the Christian standard. It is from Calvary alone that we 'know love' (1 John 3.16); only at Calvary are love's deepest dimensions understood. That is why the command to imitate Christ's love is 'new' (John 13.34). Such love was undreamed-of before.

Love is fundamental to fellowship, for fellowship consists precisely of giving and taking, and only those who love as Jesus did can give of themselves in the way that fellowship requires.

In the 1 John passage the apostle casts this commandment, as he does so much else, into a test of life. He who does not love his brother (i.e. his fellow Christian) is thereby shown to be a child, not of God, but of the devil (10–12). Like Cain, and the world generally (13), he hates godly men because they make him feel uncomfortable, and hate is murder before God (cf. Matt. 5.21 f.) whether it breaks out in murderous action or not (15). John's antithesis is inexorable and ultimately inescapable: if you do not love, then you hate.

John adds two practical points. The first concerns assurance. From finding in ourselves love of the brethren, we know by infallible inference, that we have passed from spiritual death to spiritual life—for one cannot love all Christians as such without being spiritually alive (14). The second point detects hypocrisy. Love is more than talk; it is action for the relief of need (17 f.). Only action of this kind is love 'in truth' (i.e. reality) (18).

80 : Sharing

Acts 2.43–47; 4.32–37

Pentecost loosed into the world a new quality of corporate life, marked by an exuberant riot of caring and sharing and an infectious joy (2.46), which overthrew all inhibitions about going to the limit to help others. This was *fellowship* (2.42)—*koinonia*, literally 'having things in common'. In v. 46, '*generous* hearts' (RSV) is a good interpretation of 'singleness'—single-minded concentration on giving, as a mark of love, is the meaning intended. Though spontaneous in expression, the new life-style was not uncaused: it issued from the Spirit's new covenant ministry, making the love and power of Christ vividly real. Fellowship between Christians always comes about through conscious realization of Christ's own fellowship with each of them (cf. 1 John 1.3).

As praise is both a Christian instinct (2.47) and a duty, so with togetherness (cf. 2.44; 4.32). Heb. 3.13; 10.24 f., present meeting and mutual ministry as a duty, but here togetherness in worship, at table and at other times (2.46 f.), is recorded simply as a fact. The RSV is right in 4.23 to interpret 'their own people' (the literal meaning) as 'friends': that is how Christians saw each other in those days of spiritual vigour, and friends do not usually need to be told to get together!

The ancient world by and large was callous towards poverty, but the first practical expression of Christian fellowship was to pool resources for poor relief (2.45; 4.32, 34 ff.). For the first time ever Marx's maxim, 'From each according to his ability; to each according to his need', became the rule of action. The maxim, which came to Marx from Christian sources, is, of course, profoundly right, but only where Christ is Lord can there be motive force enough to live it out. The poverty of the Jerusalem saints twenty-five years later (cf. Rom. 15.25–27) may suggest that from one standpoint this experiment in communal Christianity was injudicious: it may have reflected an incautious assumption that because Jesus' return is certain (cf. Acts 3.20) therefore it must be soon (cf. the Thessalonian mistake, 2 Thess. 2.1 f.; 3.6–12). Paul's charge to the rich (1 Tim. 6.17 ff.) shows that there is another way of being a faithful steward of property than selling up. But the Christian good-heartedness of Barnabas, who sold his entire estate for charity, is not to be faulted; it is a model for us all (4.36 f.).

106

81 : Welcome!

Romans 15.1–13

The gospel invitation to mankind is, in the words of a Bunyan book title, 'come and welcome to Jesus Christ'. The Church's invitation to believers must always be, 'come and welcome into the fellowship of those whom Christ has welcomed' (7).

In Rom. **14.1**–**15.13**, Paul argues that Christians must receive each other with the same full acceptance, the same concern for the other's welfare, and the same forbearance of the other's weaknesses, as Christ showed in receiving them. So we must bear with each other's oddities and scruples about food and drink, Sabbath-keeping, and other areas where Christian liberty and discretion come in (**14.1**–12); we must not let our freedom be another's stumbling-block (**14.13**–23); like Christ, the archetypal Servant (**15.8**), we must forgo the luxury of pleasing ourselves, so that our neighbour may be edified and God's cause maintained (2 f.). Jew and Gentile in particular must fully receive each other in Christ, for Scripture is explicit that Christ came to save both (7–13).

It is worth asking how this bears on (*a*) racially or sociologically selective congregations and (*b*) intercommunion between denominational groups.

As Paul develops his theme, three other truths come in as a kind of bass line:

1. *Scripture's purpose is to encourage Christians*. Having cited Psa. **69.9** in v. 3, and intending to cite Psa. **18.49**; Deut. **32.43**; Psa. **117.1**; and Isa. **11.10** (vs. 9–12), to show that Jesus' ministry to the Gentiles was foretold no less than His rejection by the Jews, Paul is led to make the great generalization of v. 4. He spoke of the Old Testament only; how much more do his words fit the New! To show us Christ and God's promises (8) for our encouragement is the basic use of the whole Bible.

2. *Christian character is God's gift*: steadfastness, courage, hope, joy, peace, faith (5, 13) come through the word (4) and Spirit (13) alone.

3. *The goal of grace is the praise of God*, by those to whom grace came (6, 7, 9, 11, cf. Eph. **1.6**, 12, 14). So now; so for ever.

Nor are these truths irrelevant to the main theme; for Christian welcoming will be most in evidence where the giving of God is best known, and the worship of God best practised.

82 : Burden-bearing

Galatians 6.1–6

Having in ch. 5 told his readers to walk in the Spirit and serve each other in love (5.16, 25, 13 f.), Paul here explains what this will mean. The law of Christ, he says, is precisely this—to bear others' burdens (2), accepting involvement in their troubles and laying oneself out to help, support and restore (1). It pleases God more that I should carry someone else's burden and let him carry mine than that we should each carry our own. The latter is the way of lonely isolation, one aspect of the fallen human condition; the former is the way of Christian fellowship. Fellowship means sharing burdens as well as benefits: we carry each other's luggage, both material and spiritual, and find relief and strength in doing so. This path of exchange—problem-sharing and burden-bearing—is Christ's image in our lives, for it reflects His loving substitution for us under judgement on the cross. *'O Christ, what burdens bowed Thy head; my load was laid on Thee.'*

Paul summons his readers to the burden-bearing life as his *brothers* in Christ (in 4.19 he had called them his children!) and as *spiritual* men, indwelt and led by the Spirit of God. It is to this life of fellowship in action that sonship in God's family commits us (cf. 1 Pet. 3.8), and for this that the Spirit is given to equip us.

Paul weaves together two lines of exhortation: with the call to burden-bearing goes a warning against complacent conceit (1b, 3–5). Psychologically this is shrewd; those who seek to do good (10), especially in counselling and rescue work (1), are always tempted to feel they are a cut above those they are helping. 'Gentleness', as distinct from the overbearing attitude which betrays superiority feelings, is called for here, since 'there but for the grace of God go I' (cf. v. 1; 1 Cor. 10.12). Paul reminds us that the 'load' each man must carry (nothing to do with the burden-bearing of v. 2) is his responsibility for his own life, for which he must answer to God, to reap what he has sown (5, 7 ff.); so each of us will be wise to 'test his own work' (4), and not rest in the thought that some are a lot worse than he is.

The injunction of v. 6, so comforting to preachers, is not as isolated from Paul's theme as it looks. How else, when pastors are impoverished (and they often are), should the rule of burden-bearing be applied?

83 : Love that Hurts

1 Thessalonians 2.17–3.10

Following a three-week mission Paul left his Thessalonian converts in a hurry, for the Jews and the mob were demonstrating against him (Acts 17.1–10). The circumstances made persecution certain, and though Paul had told them to expect this (3.4) he feared that, being young in the faith and as yet imperfectly instructed (10) they would not have resources to cope with it (3). So he soon sent Timothy to them from Athens to support and strengthen them (1 f.). Timothy brought back good news of them—Paul's verb in v. 6 is that which he normally uses for preaching the 'good news' of the gospel—and Paul, in joy, at once wrote the letter from which this passage comes. (Incidentally, it should be read as one paragraph; the chapter division is inappropriate.) It is worth remembering that Paul's readers were perhaps a year old in the faith, but hardly more.

Pastoral love, whereby an older Christian feels and carries responsibility for other and particularly for younger Christians, is one of the costliest forms of Christian fellowship. All Christians will have some such responsibility; pastoral love is regularly required of us all, not just of ministers in pastorates. Pastoral love brings deep concern and makes one deeply vulnerable: not being able to meet those whom one loves (2.17 f.; 3.6, 10), not knowing how they are managing under pressure (5), not knowing even whether one's love is returned (6; cf. 2 Cor. 6.11–13; 12.14 f.), hurts. As a rule, those who love most are hurt most. There is, of course, another side: pastoral love blossoms into joy and pride when the loved ones make progress (2.19 f.; 3.8), and the more love the more joy. Paul knows that it is God, not himself, whom he must thank for his converts' faith and faithfulness (7–9; 1.2); but the joy he has in the knowledge that he has not, under God, laboured in vain (3.5) is real and honest and nothing to be ashamed of 'before our God' (9). To know that God has used you to bless others in a decisive way, is joy indeed.

So far from exploiting the loved ones in its own interest, pastoral love identifies with their interests and is all at their disposal. So Paul prays, and is ready to work again, for his converts' spiritual welfare (10–13; 2.18; 1.2). It is to encourage them that Paul sweetly tells them how the news of their steadfastness had ministered encouragement to him (7 f.).

84 : The Way of Fellowship

1 John 1

John's first letter is the classic New Testament treatment of fellowship. Two paragraphs form its first chapter. Verses 1–4 are John's *preamble*, stating why he is writing; vs. 5–10 give his *principles*, which determine the letter's content. 'That you may have fellowship with us' is the purpose (3), and the principles are these:

Axiom—God is wholly *light*; that is, purity and holiness are what He is, what He demands, and what He gives (5). (In the way that He gives it He shows Himself to be love too [4.8–10].) Hence follow four corollaries:

1. Those who walk (live) in darkness (impurity and unholiness) have no fellowship with God (6).

2. Those who walk in the light enjoy fellowship with each other and cleansing, through Christ before God, so that nothing disrupts traffic between them and Him (7).

3. Those who deny their sins are truth-less and self-deceived, contradicting God (8, 10).

4. Those who acknowledge their sins receive forgiveness and cleansing from God (9).

The rest of the letter rings changes on these principles.

Fellowship with God for John is a love-traffic of receiving from Him and giving to Him. We enter it through receiving apostolic witness to Christ (1.3, 5), which the Spirit enables us to do (2.20, 27). John elucidates the relationship in terms of:

(*a*) *Living*: having 'life', 'the life', 'that eternal life' which is in Jesus the Son, and which indeed Jesus Himself is (1.1 f.; 5.11–13, 20).

(*b*) *Knowing* God, Father and Son (1.3; 5.20), and the love of both (4.16, 3.16). This involves acknowledging the realities of the Son's incarnation as Jesus the Christ (4.2) and His atoning death ('blood') (1.7, cf. 2.2; 4.9 f.)—otherwise one 'has' neither the Son nor the Father (2.22 f.).

(*c*) *Loving* God for His love, and so obeying and abiding in Him (2.5, 15; 4.19; 5.2 f.).

(*d*) *Receiving* God's gifts in answer to prayer (3.22; 5.14–16).

Fellowship with Christians means loving them in a practical way (3.18)—providing for their needs (3.17), and praying for them (cf. 5.16). It is a relationship presupposing personal fellowship with the Father and the Son on the part of each individual involved (1.3).

Questions and themes for study and discussion on Studies 79-84

1. In what ways does the command, 'Love one another as I have loved you', mark an advance on Old Testament ethics?
2. In the light of Study 80, how far should a church go in looking after the material needs of its members?
3. How can one love and live in fellowship with persons of a different background to oneself, whom one does not like?
4. Think out ways in which the principle of bearing one another's burdens can and should be applied.
5. Can one be in fellowship with another Christian without having thereby some pastoral responsibility for him?
6. What does it mean to 'walk in the light'?

CHARACTER STUDIES

85 : Peter

Mark 14.17–31; John 13.1–20, 36–38

John alone records the events which preceded the breaking of the bread at the supper in the Upper Room—probably a rooftop structure on the house of John Mark's mother. The quarrel which had marred the walk up from Jericho on the long dusty road had not subsided (Luke 22.24–30). The ritual of foot-washing had been disregarded. They had no servants, and the humble duty of fetching water, and thus helping each other, had gone by the board in the heat of their contention over precedence. It is difficult to imagine the pain the Lord endured as He sought to shame them from their sin by taking the duty upon Himself.

Peter's outburst of love is typical—unwise, unreasoning but surging up from a loyal, devoted heart. It shows that he, at least, was humbled and broken by what his Master had done. John omits the story of the Supper itself, but tells again of Peter's expression of loyalty and the Lord's sad reply. He knew what Judas was doing. He knew that the hour was near. He could easily plot the course of events till sunrise. And He knew what was in poor Peter.

Mark, so brief in much else, reports the Lord's prediction to Peter in fuller fashion than the rest: 'Before the cock crows twice, you will deny me three times.' Travellers in Palestine in the last century, before the modern revival of the land obliterated ancient patterns of events, are said to have noted the frequency of two periods of night-time cock-crowing. Peter's three denials were thus punctuated by the warning of the first sounding of the cock. Others say that 'cockcrow' was the first bugle call from the Roman garrison barracks. The poignant touch in the story is this: Peter, according to tradition, was Mark's authority for his account. He must have directed his friend to tell the whole truth about him, realizing that the best use he could make of his deep shame was to turn it into warning, and with it block the path of others' stumbling. Peter was no Judas. In spite of His sad prophecy, the Lord looked at the surge of love and loyalty which had prompted the confident assertion. He knew that Peter had been moved by the strange symbolism of the Supper, and stirred to concern by the reference to betrayal. Verse 31 is pathetically emphatic. It runs literally: 'He kept saying with the utmost vehemence. Even if I die by your side, I shall certainly not deny you.'

86 : Judas

Luke 22.1–6; John 12.1–8

There has been much speculation over Judas' motives. He was the one member of the band who was not a Galilean. Perhaps he had built up some notion of rejection, of unpopularity or resentment, against the closer knit society of the rest. Perhaps he had so set his heart on earthly position in some imagined concept of the coming Kingdom, that he could not endure the disillusionment when it became apparent that Christ's Kingdom was not of this world. Resentfully he began to embezzle to reimburse himself. Or did he think to put Christ to the final test, to drive Him to use His power by confronting Him with dire peril or with death? He could have perversely argued that this test would solve his own bitter problem. If the Lord did nothing, fell into captivity, died, then Judas would have proved to himself that his years of discipleship had indeed been wasted, that he was rid of an impostor or a visionary. On the other hand, if the last challenge provoked divine response, then he, Judas, had set the machinery in motion. So he may have argued.

Disloyalty was of long standing and long carefully concealed. As far back as the events of John 6.70 f. the Lord had been aware of a traitor in the midst, and had openly expressed His knowledge. It was, it seems, subsequent to this knowledge that He made him treasurer of the poor funds of the little band, as though to appeal to the covetous man by an act of confidence and trust. By the time of which we read in John 12, Judas had become an embittered man. He saw no beauty in Mary's sacrifice, no pathos in the knowledge it expressed. He saw only that which he had fitted himself to see. His bent mind could see only through the veil of its own distortions.

Truth rejected is dangerous. Judas had lived in the presence of Christ. He had hardened his heart against all appeal. Somewhere, somehow, he had been disappointed. At that point he should have examined his life, faced his own inadequacies, and opened heart and mind to a loftier call. Instead he cherished evil, and it grew like a cancer until it ate up its host. But Judas was no monster at the beginning. It is what man accepts in the heart's depth that determines what man becomes.

87 : Judas Again

John 13.21–35; Psalm 41.9

Judas had chosen, but the Lord did not give him up. Three separate appeals, unnoticed by the uncomprehending men round the table, are visible in this story. Sixty years later John could look back and recognize their significance. Girded with the linen towel, Christ washed Judas' feet along with those of the rest. He must have looked up into the hard determined face and read the worst there was to read. Judas was past the point of recall.

Then He must have asked Judas to sit beside Him. Otherwise the conversation recorded would have been impossible. They reclined at table, and it is a fair guess that John was on one side of his Master, Judas on the other. How else could He have conveniently spoken to him or handed him 'the sop'?

And consider the sop. It was (and is still among the Arabs) a custom to pass a choice morsel to a favoured guest. Judas was singled out for this attention . . . Three times, then, the Lord marked with special favour the one whom He knew to be a traitor. He was unable to touch him. Judas was quite determined on his sin. His play-acting must have been cynically perfect, because he knew that the Lord was aware of his betrayal. He was playing with skill a dangerous part.

He was not bidden go and do his grim deed until every possible opportunity to repent had been set before him. The fact that he was not unmasked was itself an appeal, because Judas must have known full well how precarious his safety would have been had the others of the band been plainly told about his treachery. John only had some inkling . . .

Inkling enough to feel with peculiar sharpness the significance of the moment. Judas went out, 'and it was night', wrote John, an old man now in distant Ephesus. But everyone, who had followed the story or read it in the other evangelists, knew that it was night. Why the phrase? John, deeply aware that evil was afoot, and that Judas was at the centre of it, saw the door open, and the traitor disappear. He was never, all his long life, able to forget that sudden oblong of darkness. It seemed so hideously appropriate as Judas stepped into it. Such touches mark the work of the eye-witness.

Questions and themes for study and discussion on Studies 85–87

1. 'You call me Master and Lord, and so I am . . .'
2. The mind of Judas. Can any man play his part?
3. The divine pursuit of rebellious man, and this theme in Francis Thompson's poem *The Hound of Heaven*.

LIFE IN CHRIST

The Christian in the World

88 : Be Different

Deuteronomy 6.10–15; 12.29–32

God's world, having rejected its Maker, is always at cross purposes with His people. This must be frankly faced; we dare not be starry-eyed about it. Such was Moses' message to Israel, standing poised to enter Canaan. In Canaan, he says, you will be tempted to become like the locals, and like your neighbours, but you are called to be nonconformists—indeed, separatists!—in relation to these things. Be different! or the God who is cutting off the Canaanites in judgement before you (12.29) will turn and destroy you as well (6.15).

Moses, like all good preachers, has three points:

1. *Don't forget the Lord* (6.12). He is a great and gracious benefactor (10 f.), a strong Saviour (12), and as He remembers His promise to give (10) so He expects us to remember our obligation to serve (12 f.). Sin and Satan, however, create absent-mindedness where God's deeds and claims are concerned (cf. Matt. 13.19; Jer. 2.32; 3.21; 13.25; 18.15). Today's pressures quickly obliterate the memory of yesterday's provision, and the very enjoyment of God's good gifts can divert our hearts from the Giver (10 ff.). The constant commemoration of God's works in the Psalms is a deliberate antidote to this (cf. Pss. 42.6; 77.11 f.; 105 5)—and such antidotes are always in season. The Passover and Lord's Supper were instituted as antidotes against forgetfulness, too (cf. Deut. 16.3; 1 Cor. 11.24 ff.).

2. *Don't divide your loyalty* (6.14). As a loving husband is rightly jealous that his wife's affection should be exclusively his, and will be justly angry if she plays him false, so with God (15). God's people, therefore, must play the faithful wife's role and keep themselves wholly for Him, as the first commandment requires (5.7; 6.4 f.). The 'fear' they must practise is, as always in Scripture, a combination of reverence, loyalty and love in response to covenant mercy (13). Swearing by God's name is a way of showing allegiance (13). (Jesus' attack on the mentality

that covers deceit with oaths [Matt. 5.33–37] does not contradict this; it is a different point.)

3. *Don't serve God in pagan ways* (12.30 f.). Barbarities which God hates in the service of superstition would be equally hateful in His own worship. It is obedience, not sacrifice (let alone human sacrifice) that He wants (32; cf. 1 Sam. 15.22). So curb your conformist cravings, attend to His word, and—be different!

89 : Salt and Light

Matthew 5.13–16; Ephesians 5.3–14

Jesus uses two parables (comparisons, illustrations) to show what influence His disciples should have in the world. First, the parable of *salt* (Matt. 5.13) teaches that they are to act as a preservative and a flavouring: that is, they should be a force making against rottenness and for wholeness in sin-sick society. This requires them to be *in* the world, not withdrawn from it (cf. John 17.15; 1 Cor. 5.10); for salt cannot preserve what it does not touch. It requires also that they be *different* from the world, for only so can they fulfil their own regenerate nature and do their appointed job. Salt that has lost its saltness is a useless mockery of itself: it is fit only to be thrown away. Finally, Jesus' figure suggests that Christians need not be discouraged when in a minority: a little real salt will preserve a lot of meat!

The parable of *light* teaches four main truths. First, God means the Christian community to be noticed. Just by existing, it should be calling attention to itself, like a city on a hill (14); if men can overlook it, something is wrong! Second, God means this community to enlighten the world. By being itself, and living its own life, it is to expose the shoddiness and unworthiness of the world's ways and display in practice what human existence is meant to be. Lights are not lit so that they may then be stopped from shining! (14 f.). Third, the community must be zealous and untiring in the practice of 'good works' (16, cf. Tit. 2.14): 'let your light shine'. Fourth, the community's exhibition of the Christian way of life is meant to move others to praise their God— and once people have begun to praise the Christian God for others' salvation, they may well before long be found going to Him to seek their own (16). Note that there is no disjunction here between deeds and words as alternative ways of witness, as the

117

'silent service' tend to suppose ('I witness by my life, not by talking'); Jesus' assumption is rather that verbal witness to the Christians' heavenly Father has already been borne (how else would watching worldlings know to praise Him?), and the 'good works' are now backing it up.

The Ephesians passage follows a parallel line of thought: 1. As light in the Lord, *avoid* the darkness of the world's ways (3–10). 2. As light in the Lord, *expose* that darkness (11 ff.), as your own new way of life cannot but do (9 f.). 3. As light in the Lord, you will thus *arouse* those who sleep in that darkness to receive the light of Christ (13 f.).

90 : Against Men

Matthew 10.16–42

This passage, the end of Jesus' charge to the twelve setting out to preach in Galilee (10.5 ff.), looks on to situations which would only develop later, when following post-Pentecostal clashes with the authorities serious persecution of Christians by their fellow Jews would start (cf. Acts 8.1 ff.). Three themes appear: do not trust men, but trust God (16–25); do not fear men, but fear God (26–33); do not follow your family, but follow Christ (34–42). Each section ends by focusing on Jesus' own place and ministry: first, as the divine Master whose lot His servants must be ready to share (24 f.); second, as the divine Son who in heaven will champion before His Father those who championed Him on earth (32 f.); third, as the divine Emissary who is received, as the God who sent Him is received, when His own representatives are received, and who will see that those who receive them are rewarded (40 ff.). Jesus' awareness of being Son of God, sent to be men's Teacher, King and Judge, is explicit here.

The first section says that disciples must be prepared for hatred (22) and persecution (17 f., 22 f., 25). Men will be 'wolves' for ferocity in opposing them (16), for the preaching of the gospel raises the antithesis between the world and God to its height. But the Spirit is promised for their defence, so they should not panic (19 f.). Verse 23 is enigmatic; perhaps Jesus meant it so. His coming to the throne through the ascension, of which evidence was given at Pentecost (cf. 26.64=Luke 22.69), or His coming to Jerusalem in judgement in A.D. 70 are both easier reference-points for the last phrase than is the Second Coming.

The second section says that disciples must not be daunted from proclaiming Christ by fear of men (26, 28, 31). For (a) God means the secret of the gospel to be blazoned abroad, so that its publishers are entirely in God's will (26 f.); (b) human foes cannot in any case kill the soul (28; the second half of the verse refers to God—not the devil!); (c) God knows and can protect disciples fully (29 f.); (d) Jesus will welcome faithful witnesses into glory (32 f.).

The third section says that disciples must expect division about Christ to invade their families, creating a clash of loyalties in which for Jesus' sake they must count the family as foes (34 ff.). This is painful: but no limit can be set to what a disciple must be ready to lose and suffer on the road to his reward (37 ff.).

91 : The Secret of Stickability

Hebrews 10.32–39; 12.1–4

Christians need 'stickability'—resilience, endurance, perseverance, patience (10.36; 12.1; verb, 12.2, 3)—for they live under constant pressure from the world around. Here, Jews and worldlings had put the boot in, and the Hebrew believers were pressed hard (32 ff.). As we noted earlier (Study 39) they were tempted to think that by abandoning their Christian profession and reverting to Judaism they could gain immunity without loss. This, however, was not so: those who give up Christ (29) lose everything, for they incur the black guilt and awful judgement of apostasy (26–31, cf. 6.4–8). The letter was written to explain this to them, and to urge them to stand firm. Chapter 10.32–39 encourages them to keep on as they have been going, points to the promise of reward for those who patiently endure, and expresses confidence that they will qualify for that reward when Christ comes.

You need endurance, says the writer, and the secret of endurance is faith (35, 38 f.). He cites Hab. 2.3 f. to show that faith —meaning confident, hopeful trust in God and His promises (35, 38 f.; 11.1, 6)—is that by which the godly man will live. Paul quotes Habakkuk's words to focus the thought that a man comes to be righteous (right) with God, and so to gain life, by receiving God's gift of righteousness through Christ (Rom. 1.17; Gal. 3.11); the anonymous writer to the Hebrews uses them to show that the godly man gains life by hoping in God's promise of reward through Christ. It should be noticed that faith, in Hebrews, includes what Paul distinguishes as hope, while faith, in Paul, includes what Hebrews distinguish as confidence (10.35). The implications of Habakkuk's statement in context are broad enough to justify both Paul's use of it and that in Hebrews.

As faith is the secret of endurance, so gazing at Jesus is the secret of faith. This is the point of 12.1–4. The Christian life is pictured as a race. To run it with endurance, we must first *lay aside* every 'weight' (retarding factor) and 'clinging sin' (i.e. unbelief, sluggishness, complacency: cf. 3.12 f.; 4.11; 6.12), and then *look above* to Jesus. He is faith's pioneer and trail-blazer, in that He took this road before us, and He is its perfecter (i.e., its perfect instance) in that He maintained confident hope of joyful resurrection and enthronement through shame and suffering greater than any that face His servants (2 ff., cf. 5.7–9). And as His example now inspires our faith, so His help and strength support it (2.18, 4.15 f.).

92 : The New Life-style

1 Peter 2.9–12; 4.3–6

Christians have a new *life* (2.9 f.). 'Called' by God from the 'darkness' of ungodliness into the 'light' of knowing Christ and salvation, they have 'received mercy' (wholly contrary to merit!) and become God's people. Now their task is that of priests, appearing before God to proclaim by praise and testimony what wonders He has done for them and can do for others. Peter echoes Exod. 19.5 f. and applies its thoughts to the Israel of the new exodus and the new covenant.

Christians must therefore have a new *life-style*, rooted in knowledge of two things. First, they do not belong in this world. Heaven is their home, and here they are only 'resident aliens' (persons without rights or legal status) and 'temporary dwellers' (11, cf. Heb. 11.13, where the thought is exactly the same). Their involvement in the world must therefore rest on, and be consistent with, clear-headed detachment from it. Second, self-indulgent and potentially vicious natural appetites are not the Christian's real self, whatever may have been true before conversion, and if given rein they ruin his spiritual health (11).

So with self-disciplined restraint Christians must say 'No!' to the ways of the world and the flesh, and stand apart from the wild company with which they previously identified (4.3 f.). Instead, they must maintain the practice of 'good works' (being good and doing good—'good conduct' [2.12 RSV] gets the idea). This will shame their critics—Christians always have critics —into recognition that God is in truth working in their lives, and so prepare the way for the critics' conversion (4.4; 2.12). Conversion, rather than the judgement of 4.5, 17 f., seems to be the 'visitation' in view here, for Peter is echoing Matt. 5.16 (on which see Study 89).

Chapter 4.6 is hard, but the least difficult interpretation understands it as clearing up a difficulty due to the fact that death is God's judgement on sin. Christians who have died will be shown at the judgement to be alive to God. On this point some early Christians, we know, were uncertain, cf. 1 Thess. 4.13 ff. Peter's purpose in v. 6 is then to ward off this uncertainty, lest his readers assume that the death of the 'dead' in v. 5 was proof that they were lost.

93 : On being Unsinkable

1 Peter 4.12–19

The word *suffering* covers a multitude of experiences, physical, mental and spiritual, from bereavement and a bad conscience to toothache and torture. Suffering in some form is every man's lot in this fallen and out-of-joint world (cf. Rom. 8.18–22), and the real 'problem of suffering' is the practical problem, how can we so handle it that it becomes a stepping-stone which takes us on rather than a stumbling-block which brings us down? Suffering enriches some and destroys others; the difference reflects what one brings to it. Christianity contains a secret which can make all suffering an enrichment, and this Peter discloses to Christians facing persecution (12).

Suffering Christians share Christ's sufferings (13). That is the secret! This can be said, not only of ill-treatment occasioned by our Christian profession (14, 16), but of all sufferings whatever (cf. Rom. 8.17), apart from legal punishment for crime or antisocial action, which Christians, Peter hopes, will not incur (15). As Jesus' experiences of temptation covered and transcended

121

ours (cf. Heb. 2.18; 4.15), so with His experiences of frustration, pain, hardship, unfairness, cruelty, and the desolations of dying (cf. Heb. 5.7 ff.); and as His sufferings in His own person led Him straight to glory, so will His sufferings in us lead us who are His (12; cf. 1.6–11; Luke 24.26; Rom. 8.17). For both King and subjects, tribulation is the appointed road to the Kingdom; to be on that road authenticates one's Christianity (14), just as standing firm under pressure proves the quality of one's faith (12, cf. 1.6 f.).

Suffering with Christ, then, is to be expected (12). Knowing what we do of its significance, we can rejoice in it (13: the verb is in the present tense, and means 'keep on rejoicing'). Recognizing it as a sign of blessing, we are to praise God, count it a privilege, and bear up, trusting our faithful Creator (14–16, 19).

Verses 17 f. introduce a sobering thought from a different angle. 'If God, the righteous Judge, so hates evil, and must deal with it, that He judges His redeemed people, what will be the fate of unbelievers, when His full wrath against sinners is revealed?' (A. M. Stibbs).

94 : Against the Devil

1 Peter 5.6–11; Ephesians 6.10–20

His Hebrew name (Satan) means 'adversary'; his Greek name (*diabolos*) means 'slanderer', 'evil speaker'. He is meaner, more cruel, and more destructive than anything we can imagine. He is a fallen angel kept for judgement (Jude 6); none the less, his present power warrants calling him ruler and god of this world (John 14.30; 2 Cor. 4.4). At the cross he was 'cast out' (John 12.31), yet, though beaten, he is still fighting. His first enemy is God; he wants to thwart, spoil and bring to ruin everything God undertakes. So he fights Christians, because they are on God's side. Seeking to destroy God's work in their lives, he manipulates their circumstances and thoughts, so that their life becomes a series of 'temptations' aimed at their weak spots; and he never gives up. He is as fierce as a hungry lion (1 Pet. 5.8), and utterly deceitful (Eph. 6.11). Such is the biblical profile of 'your adversary the devil.'

What are we to do about him? Both Peter and Paul tell us to *resist* him (1 Pet. 5.9; Eph. 6.13, cf. Jas. 4.7: the same Greek verb is used each time). Jesus' reaction when He detected that suggestions had come from Satan was to say 'No!'—'Get behind me, Satan' (Matt. 16.23, cf. 4.10)—and we must react the same way. Peter puts this point in the context of submitting to God (6), trusting His care (7), exercising self-control and being on guard (8), and standing firm in faith as troubles come (9). Paul builds up his famous picture of infantryman's armour given us by God to fit us for successful resistance—the belt, which is truth known; the breastplate, which is integrity followed; the shoes, namely readiness for action given by the gospel (or, perhaps, to serve the gospel); the shield, namely faith, by which Satan's 'fiery darts' (thoughts inducing despair) are deflected; the helmet, which is salvation known, the content of assurance; and the sword, which is God's message, His promise and command, which we must use against Satan as Jesus did in the wilderness (Matt. 4.1 ff.). Prayer too, Paul adds, is vital (Eph. 6.18).

We are to take Satan seriously, but not too seriously. For all his ferocity and cunning, Christ has conquered him, and we never need yield to him. Fight in God's way, say Peter and Paul, and God will see to it that you win (1 Pet. 5.9 f.; Eph. 6.11,13).

95 : This Way to Glory

Revelation 1.9–11; 2.8–11; 7.9–17

This world is the first of two which all men successively inhabit. The book of the Revelation, a product of persecution, written under the shadow of death (1.9 ff., 2.10) and dealing with the Church's conflict between Christ's two comings—the war of the kingdoms of this world, we might say, with the Kingdom of God (cf. 1.9; 11.15; 12.10)—maintains this two-world perspective throughout. Whether our experience of the second world will take the form of 'the second death' (2.11) or 'the crown of life' (2.10) is decided here on earth. Those who live 'in Jesus' (1.9, RSV), standing for the word of God (the gospel) and witnessing to Jesus, will enjoy what they have come most to desire with Jesus hereafter (7.15–17). Others will enjoy nothing hereafter (20.11–15); God's heaven would not be heaven to them, and in any case they will not be there. As in Revelation, so throughout the New Testament, these are the issues of eternity.

These passages depict the Christian's life on earth as *tribulation for Jesus*. 'Tribulation', meaning 'pressure', 'oppression', appears as the present experience of John (1.9), the immediate prospect for Smyrna (2.10), and the launching-pad of all the great multitude clothed in white (7.9, 14). As this company is probably the whole Church, so 'the great tribulation' (14) is more likely to be a generalized description of the whole gospel age than a limited reference to one particular climax of conflict (cf. 3.10). Satan and men on his string mount the tribulation (2.10), and by inflicting death seem to triumph; but theirs is not the last word.

For these passages also depict the Christian's life in heaven as *joy through Jesus*. Faithfulness maintained under pressure is true victory, and this is the conqueror's crown of reward (2.10 f.). Those in heaven are *completely cleansed* (Christ's red, shed blood washes their robes white—a glowing paradox) (7.14); they are *in God's presence always* (15, 'throne' and 'temple' signify a sense of God as present, potent, and adorable); they know *total contentment*, free from all that hurts (16); *Jesus cares for them constantly* (note, it is the Lamb, our sacrifice, who becomes our shepherd—another glowing paradox, 17, RSV); and *God turns all bitter memories into joy* (17b). Yes!—this will really happen.

John's radiant symbolism gives us, if not a literal preview, at least a faint flavour of 'the saints' everlasting rest', of which Richard Baxter sang:

> *My knowledge of that life is small,*
> *The eye of faith is dim;*
> *But it's enough that Christ knows all*
> *And I shall be with Him.*

Yes . . . exactly.

Questions and themes for study and discussion on Studies 88–95

1. List ways in which Christians ought to be different from the world around them.
2. How far is your church fulfilling Christ's command to be 'salt' and 'light'? What are the hindrances? How can they be overcome?
3. What biblical principles should guide the Christian when members of the family, parents and spouse, even, oppose his (or her) allegiance to Christ?
4. 'Laying aside every weight.' How much does 'weight' cover? How should one determine what falls under this heading?

5. Is 'detached involvement' the proper Christian attitude to the world? If not, what is? What does 'the world' mean in this connection? To what behaviour-pattern will the proper attitude lead?

6. A Christian comes straight from the doctor to tell you that he has diagnosed inoperable cancer. What do you say?

7. 'Is it right to ascribe to Satan the promptings of our own sinful nature and silliness?' Resolve this question from Scripture.

8. How can we form meaningful ideas of heaven? What effect should thoughts of heaven have on everyday living?